DEPRESSION AMERICA

DEPRESSION AMERICA

Volume 6

THE WAR YEARS AND ECONOMIC BOOM

GROLIER
EDUCATIONAL

About This book

The Great Depression is one of the most important periods of modern U.S. history. Images of breadlines and hungry families are as haunting today as they were at the time. Why did the crisis occur in the world's richest country, and how has it shaped the United States today? *Depression America* answers these questions and reveals a highly complex period in great detail. It describes the uplifting achievements of individuals, tells touching stories of community spirit, and illustrates a rich cultural life stretching from painting to movie-making.

Each of the six volumes covers a particular aspect of the period. The first traces the causes of the Depression through the preceding decades of U.S. history. The second examines the first term of Franklin D. Roosevelt and the New Deal he put in place to temper the effects of the crisis. The third volume studies how the Depression affected the lives of ordinary Americans. Volume 4 reveals the opposition FDR faced from both the political right and left, while Volume 5 explores the effect of the period on U.S. society and culture. The final volume places the Depression in the context of global extremism and the outbreak of World War II, the effects of which restored the United States to economic health.

Each book is split into chapters that explore their themes in depth. References within the text and in a See Also box at the end of each chapter point you to related articles elsewhere in the set, allowing you to further investigate topics of particular interest. There are also many special boxes throughout the set that highlight particular subjects in greater detail. They might provide a biography of an important person, examine the effect of a particular event, or give an eyewitness account of life in the Depression.

If you are not sure where to find a subject, look it up in the set index in each volume. The index covers all six books, so it will help you trace topics throughout the set. A glossary at the end of each book provides a brief explanation of important words and concepts, and a timeline gives a chronological account of key events of the period. The Further Reading list contains numerous books and useful web sites to allow you to do your own research.

Published 2001 by Grolier Educational
Sherman Turnpike
Danbury, Connecticut 06816

© 2001 Brown Partworks Limited

Set ISBN: 0-7172-5502-6
Volume ISBN: 0-7172-5508-5

Library of Congress Cataloging-in-Publication Data
Depression America
    p. cm.
    Includes indexes
    Contents: v. 1. Boom and bust – v. 2. Roosevelt's first term – v. 3. Countryside and city – v. 4. Political tensions – v. 5. U.S. society – v. 6. The war years and economic boom.
    ISBN 0-7172-5502-6 (set : alk. paper)
    1. United States–Economic conditions–1918-1945–Juvenile literature. 3. New Deal, 1933-1939–Juvenile literature. 4. Working class–United States–Juvenile literature. 5. United States–Social life and customs–1918-1945–Juvenile literature. [1. Depressions–1929. 2. New Deal, 1933-1939. 3. United States–History–1919-1933. 4. United States–History– 1933-1945. 5. United States–Economic conditions– 1918-1945.]

HC106.3 D44 2001
330.973'0916–dc21

                                    00-046641

For information address the publisher:
Grolier Educational, Sherman Turnpike,
Danbury, Connecticut 06816

Printed and bound in Singapore

For Brown Partworks
Volume consultant:
Patrick Reagan, Tennessee Technological University
Managing editor: Tim Cooke
Editors: Claire Ellerton, Edward Horton, Christine Hatt, Lee Stacy
Designers: Sarah Williams, Lynne Ross
Picture research:
Becky Cox, Helen Simm, Daniela Marceddu
Indexer: Kay Ollerenshaw

CONTENTS

1

ECONOMICS AND POLITICAL EXTREMISM IN EUROPE AND JAPAN, 1919–1933

At the end of World War I Americans were relieved to get their fighting men back home, and as their newspapers chronicled the strife and turmoil that continued to plague the Old World, they counted their blessings and directed their attention to matters at home. However, developments in Europe and East Asia were changing the international landscape in a menacing way.

In the wake of World War I Europe was a devastated continent (see Volume 1, Chapter 2, "The United States in World War I"). The loss of life in the carnage had been appalling. Throughout the continent eight million men had been killed, with probably another two million succumbing to disease in the dreadful conditions of trench warfare. A further seven million were permanently disabled, and perhaps as many as 15 million seriously wounded. Some nations had endured particularly shattering casualty rates. France, for example, had lost close to 1.5 million men killed, with 3.5 million wounded. One estimate has put the loss of life in Germany at 15 percent of the active male population. Russia lost 1.7 million dead. In one day's fighting alone on July 1, 1916, the British army suffered over 57,000 casualties. The casualty statistics from the conflict are of such a magnitude as to be difficult to comprehend.

Delegates to the peace conference at Versailles, France (left), in 1919 draft the agreement that will shape the postwar world.

1. GERMANY IN DEFEAT

In nations like Great Britain and France there was, at least, the saving grace of victory. Germans faced the ruins and rubble in the terrible knowledge of defeat. In the last few days before the guns finally fell silent on November 11, 1918, the German emperor, Kaiser Wilhelm II, no longer buttressed by his army and his generals, slunk into exile in Holland. Amid turmoil and confusion government eventually passed into the hands of Friedrich

The funeral of Karl Liebknecht, one of the leading German revolutionaries murdered in the upheavals of January 1919.

Ebert (1871–1925), the leader of the Social Democrats, and a democratic republic was proclaimed from the balcony of the Reichstag, the German parliament in Berlin. The republic thereby created was to be forever tainted with defeat and the terms forced on Germany by the Treaty of Versailles of 1919. Throughout the 14-year existence of the Weimar Republic (named for the historic city where the new constitution was drawn up) its enemies, united in nothing else, were joined in their hatred of the peace and what they saw as the betrayal of the German army by the civilian politicians.

In the short term Ebert was obliged to call on the army to stave off social revolution. At the same time as the new democratic republic was being proclaimed from the Reichstag, the revolutionary Karl Liebknecht (1871–1919) was occupying the now empty imperial palace and proclaiming a socialist republic,

The Cost of War

The economic cost of World War I was colossal, and the economic consequences were to form a permanent backdrop to the political and social history of the years between 1919 and 1933. On the Western Front 6,000 square miles of France had been turned into a wasteland, much of it in areas that had, before the war, provided the bulk of the country's coal, iron, and other raw materials. On the Eastern Front Poland had seen 11 million acres of its agricultural land devastated and nearly two million buildings destroyed. To finance the war, both sides had incurred huge debts. Precise figures are hard to estimate, but one historian has suggested that the cost of the four years of war was "six and a half times the total national debts of the world from the end of the 18th century until 1914."

Nazi paramilitaries, members of the notorious SA, preparing to break up a communist meeting in Munich on May Day, 1923.

promising "to build a new order of the proletariat." The stage was set for violence and insurrection. Ebert managed to maintain his fragile new government until the new year and called an election for January 19, 1919. Liebknecht and others on the revolutionary left did not bother waiting for the election. On January 6 they organized a general strike and seized control of major rail stations and public buildings. Ebert was in a daze of confusion and uncertainty, but others in his government and in the army were not. The minister of defense, Gustav Noske, with the support of senior military figures, unleashed the newly created Freikorps (Free Corps) on the insurgents. Several days of brutal fighting followed. Hundreds of communists were killed, including Karl Liebknecht and his leading colleague Rosa Luxemburg; they were murdered en route to prison and their bodies hurled into a Berlin canal.

THE ROLE OF THE FREIKORPS

This was the first significant occasion on which the Freikorps played a leading role in the new Germany. It would not be the last. The Freikorps would continue to

bedevil the Weimar Republic, and its existence paved the way—and provided many of the men—for the right-wing paramilitary groups that soon emerged,

•

"…the flotsam and jetsam of the demobilizing army."

•

including the Nazi Party's militia, the SA. The Freikorps were what one historian has called "the flotsam and jetsam of the demobilizing army, which still retained their weapons and something of their corporate spirit." They became troops for hire, united in their hatred of the peace terms and of anything that smacked even slightly of communism. In some cases they degenerated into little more than bands of mercenary killers.

On two further occasions in the early days of the Weimar Republic the Freikorps played a decisive role in the political arena. In Munich a left-wing socialist, Kurt Eisner (1867–1919), had seized power as early as November 7, 1918, and had instituted a somewhat ramshackle Bavarian regime independent of the government in Berlin. In February 1919 Eisner was assassinated by a right-winger—ironically, he was on his way to resign as president of the faltering government—and chaos ensued. Further political assassinations followed, and in April 1919 a republic of Soldiers' and Workers' Councils, modeled on the Soviet example, was proclaimed.

The Freikorps mounted what was almost an invasion of Bavaria and Munich, and the new Soviet Republic was rapidly destroyed. In the process the Freikorps massacred more than 1,000 people who were, or were thought to be, communists. By early 1920 it was clear that the Freikorps, which Ebert and Noske had used to support the government, had become as big a threat to the fledgling democracy as was the far left. Noske tried to force General Walther von Lüttwitz, commander of irregular troops in Germany, to disband one of the most notorious Freikorps brigades. Lüttwitz responded by ordering the same brigade to occupy Berlin. The government fled, and a new right-wing regime was instituted. Within a week the legitimate government was back at the helm, but the putsch showed the danger the Freikorps represented.

HITLER TAKES THE STAGE

It was to a Munich under the chaotic rule of Kurt Eisner that Corporal Adolf Hitler (1889–1945)

A woman exchanges food for shoe repairs in the early 1920s, when Germany was gripped by inflation. The sign invites such barter.

Workers' Party (NSDAP), of which Nazi party was an abbreviation. It was largely as a result of Hitler's powers as a public speaker that membership in the party grew to 2,000 by the end of 1920. When, in July 1921, there was a power struggle between Drexler and Hitler, it was an unequal contest. Hitler emerged as party chairman with more or less unlimited powers.

Capitalizing on Crisis

In 1922 and 1923 the Nazi Party, galvanized by Hitler's leadership, made rapid strides. The Weimar regime seemed to totter from crisis to crisis. Catastrophic inflation made the currency almost valueless. In January 1922 one U.S. dollar bought about 190 marks. A year later the dollar was worth more than 17,500 marks. By the end of 1923 an egg cost 80 million marks and a glass of beer 150 million. National pride took a body blow in January 1923 when

returned in November 1918. He had lived there before the war, and now, released from a military hospital in Pomerania, he made his way back there. Hitler was still a member of the Reichswehr, the German army—he was not discharged until March 1920. As an observer on behalf of the Reichswehr that on September 12, 1919, he attended a political meeting of the fringe German Workers' Party. A few days later he joined the party.

The party, founded earlier in the year by Anton Drexler and Karl Harrer, had a tiny membership. It was only one of dozens of right-wing, nationalist groups that had sprung up in the aftermath of the war, all bitterly opposed to the peace and to the "November criminals" who had negotiated it. All drew support from, among others, the disenchanted soldiers who made up the Freikorps. In such a small organization as the German

Workers' Party Hitler's talents as demagogue and propagandist and the fervor of his ideological commitment were bound to bring him to the fore. By the time of the proclamation of the party's program on February 24, 1920, it was Hitler rather than Drexler or Harrer who was the voice of the tiny party. It was Hitler who announced a program that he had partly drafted himself. A week later the party changed its name to the National Socialist German

SA paramilitaries on a training march outside Munich in 1923. At this early stage Hitler thought the SA could propel the Nazis to power.

The Beer Hall Putsch

The 1923 Beer Hall Putsch was a fiasco as a military coup, but the ensuing trial of Hitler and others was turned into a major propaganda success for the National Socialists. For a small group of conspirators in Munich to bring down the national government was not as improbable an undertaking as it might seem from a distance. The idea was to entangle the state government of Bavaria, right wing and severely at odds with Berlin, in the plot and force it to authorize a march on Munich. This ensuing upheaval was to provide the spearhead for a national revolution.

On November 7, 1923, the leaders of a number of right-wing, nationalist groups, including Hitler and the veteran Field Marshal Ludendorff, met to discuss plans. Influenced by Hitler's rhetoric, the conspirators decided to act immediately. The following evening several members of the Bavarian government were to address an audience at the Bürgerbräukeller, a complex of halls and bars about half a mile from the center of Munich. The bold scheme was to invade the meeting, take the Bavarian leaders hostage, and force them to endorse the march. All went well at first. Hitler, at the head of a troop of SA men, burst into the meeting while other SA men cordoned off the buildings. Gustav von Kahr, the general state commissioner appointed by the Bavarian cabinet, his military counterpart General Otto Herman von Lassow, and Colonel Hans Ritter von Seisser, the head of the state police, were in the hands of the conspirators and, caving in to threats, pledged their support for the putsch.

At this point Hitler made the mistake of leaving the beer hall to see how operations in other parts of the city had gone. After he had left, Kahr, von Lassow, and von Seisser persuaded Ludendorff to release them. Once free of the immediate threat, all three repudiated their statements of support. On the ninth Hitler, Ludendorff, and their fellow conspirators, together with a large body of armed SA men, marched on the city. They were met by the state police, and at some point a shot rang out. This was the signal for a fusillade of shots from both sides. Sixteen Nazis were killed and hundreds wounded. Göring was shot in the groin. Hitler dislocated his shoulder falling to the ground to avoid the bullets.

Nazis menace the streets of Munich, November 9, 1923, as Hitler makes his audacious bid to topple the Bavarian government.

the French, infuriated by Germany's inability to meet reparation payments as stipulated in the Treaty of Versailles, occupied the industrial Ruhr region of western Germany in an attempt to enforce payment. In such circumstances

the appeal of a fringe party, with simplistic remedies and an array of easily identifiable scapegoats to blame for any crisis, increased. Not only did the party grow. So too did its paramilitary wing, the Sturmabteilung or SA, soon to be

under the command of Hermann Göring (1893–1946), a famous World War I air ace, who had joined the party after hearing Hitler speak. In February 1923 the SA was united with a number of other paramilitary forces in

Lining up for water supplies during a general strike in Germany in 1925. Chronic instability proved fertile ground for the Nazis.

Bavaria, and Hitler's thoughts began to turn toward an armed uprising against the hated Weimar regime. This found expression in the infamous Beer Hall Putsch of November 1923 (see box).

BATTLE FOR THE STREETS

In 1920s Germany it was not only the far right that resorted to street violence such as the Beer Hall Putsch, and not only the right that organized paramilitary groups to menace its political opponents. Communists and others on the left had their bully boys too. The German Communist Party, born out of the antiwar German Spartacist movement, was formally instituted at the beginning of 1919 by Karl Liebknecht and Rosa Luxemburg only days before their murders. Members of the party were involved in the short-lived Bavarian Soviet Republic that followed the assassination of Kurt Eisner and was so bloodily suppressed by the Freikorps. There was even a "Red Army," under the command of a 26-year-old sailor who had participated in the Kiel naval mutiny in 1918, but it proved remarkably ineffective in action. In the industrial Ruhr another large band was formed calling itself a "Red Army." It fought brutal battles against the Freikorps, which were only stopped when the French sent troops to halt such a violation of the Versailles provisions.

Like the Nazis, the communists entered the democratic process without believing in it. Communist deputies sat in the Reichstag throughout the 1920s, and their leader, Ernst Thälmann (1886–1944), contested the presidential election of 1925 after the death of Ebert and ran against Hitler and the aging war hero Field Marshal Paul von Hindenburg (1847–1934) in 1932.

In parallel to these electoral politics there was a street politics of violence and thuggery. Nazis broke up communist meetings and beat up the party's supporters. Communist groups, armed with sticks and often pistols, did the same to Nazi meetings and supporters. Throughout the late 1920s and early 1930s both sides had their martyrs. Horst Wessel was a young, middle-class recruit to the Berlin SA who became involved with a prostitute. Her pimp was a communist, and with others he invaded Wessel's apartment and killed him. The Nazi propaganda chief Josef Goebbels (1897–1945) seized on this rather squalid little personal drama and turned it into a publicity coup for the Nazis. He organized an elaborate funeral for Wessel, although it was attacked by communists and degenerated into a running street battle. He found a second-rate poem that Wessel had published in a Nazi newspaper and so promoted it that it became an anthem for the SA and for the Nazi Party as a whole.

The Nazi-communist clashes reached some kind of violent climax in the summer of 1932. The celebrated novelist and essayist Arthur Koestler, then a communist working in the Berlin publishing world, remembered that "during the long, stifling summer of 1932 we fought our ding-dong battle with the Nazis. Hardly a day passed without one or two dead in Berlin." On some occasions, and in some places, it was considerably more than one or two. On July 17, 1932, Nazi demonstrators, marching in a largely communist-controlled area of Hamburg, were shot at from windows and rooftops. They

returned fire. When the fighting had been halted, it was found that 17 people, including some members of the police caught

•

"Hardly a day passed without one or two dead in Berlin."

•

between the two sides, had been killed. With this background it was inevitable that when Hitler came to power, one of his first moves would be against the communists. Many found themselves in concentration camps. Thälmann was to end his days in Buchenwald concentration camp, shot by the SS.

HITLER'S REVISED STRATEGY
However, in the immediate aftermath of the 1923 Munich Beer Hall Putsch the chances of the Nazis ever being in a position of national power must have seemed bleak. Hitler and other leaders were under arrest. The plot had gone disastrously wrong. Yet Hitler succeeded in turning his trial for treason, which began in February 1924, into a platform for his views. On April 1 the court handed down the lenient sentence of five years' imprisonment, of which he served only nine months. He was released from Landsberg prison on December 20, 1924. While in prison Hitler composed much of his political manifesto, *Mein Kampf*, dictating it to his abjectly loyal supporter Rudolf Hess (1894–1987). He also had time to meditate on the lessons of the failed putsch. He came to the sober conclusion that armed uprising against the

The 35-year-old Hitler poses in Landsberg prison during his brief incarceration in 1924. He used the time to write Mein Kampf.

government was not the way for the Nazis to proceed. Instead, the party would use the existing democratic process to get hold of the levers of power. Once in power, the despised democracy could be dumped. This switch in strategy bore abundant fruit. In little more than eight years' time the failed revolutionary imprisoned in Landsberg was to become chancellor of Germany.

It is extremely unlikely that the Nazis would have strode to power in anything like normal circumstances. But the circumstances were anything but normal, and it took several unique and interlinked economic and political factors to pave the way for them. First was the weight of wartime reparations that hung around Germany's neck and was such a focus of national resentment that the Nazis were able to exploit. Second was the worldwide

Mein Kampf

Hitler's creed as expressed in this work is an unoriginal mishmash of radical ideas current in the Vienna of his youth. He claimed that the Aryan race, which he considered synonymous with the German people or the *Volk,* was superior to all others. To achieve their destiny, the *Volk* would need to be united under the *Führer* (leader), who, as the embodiment of the *Volk,* must have absolute authority. His will was their will, and the Nazi Party existed to implement that will.

Excitement in Nuremberg during a Nazi Party rally in 1929. The following year the Nazis made a significant electoral breakthrough.

publicity for their party. In particular it brought Hitler into contact with the immensely powerful press baron Alfred Hugenberg, whose newspapers had large circulations throughout Germany. These newspapers began to publicize Hitler and the Nazis and sing their praises as patriots. Through Hugenberg, who was also leader of a right-wing political party, Hitler began to make valuable contacts with the major figures of the "respectable" right.

NAZIS COME TO THE FORE

In October 1929 came the Wall Street Crash (see Volume 1, Chapter 6, "The Crash of 1929"), and the rippling effects of that disaster soon reached Germany, whose struggling economy had largely been sustained by

depression that struck so dramatically at the financial security of millions and seemed to discredit conventional politics and politicians. Then there was the critical factor that a small group of conservative nationalists, none of whom believed in his heart in the Weimar Republic, decided that they could use and control the upstart Hitler and his Nazi Party. This terrible miscalculation would in the end tip the scales in Hitler's favor.

REPARATIONS FUEL CRISIS

In the elections of 1928 the Nazis won only 2.8 percent of the popular vote and gained only 12 seats in the Reichstag. They remained merely a high-profile fringe party. In 1929, however, the issue of German war reparations, which had been a lingering, seemingly intractable problem throughout the 1920s, again came to the fore. Five years earlier a committee under the American financier and later vice president Charles Dawes (1865–1951) had proposed a reduction in Germany's payments, and this had

been accepted by the Allied Reparations Commission. But the Dawes Plan still seemed to many to make greater demands on Germany than its economy could take. A new committee, headed by Owen D. Young (1874–1962), met in Paris in February 1929 to seek "a final and definitive settlement" to the problem.

The Young Plan further reduced Germany's obligations, but it infuriated the German right-wing parties, who felt that any further payment was too much. In the ensuing campaign within Germany to reject the Young Plan the Nazis were able to join forces with other far-right nationalists and gain much-needed

Election poster for the German Communist Party, 1932: "Enough of this system." In fact, the system was about to be smashed.

A melee in Fiume (modern Rijeka, Croatia) as Italian adventurer Gabriele D'Annunzio is toppled from power in January 1921.

ployed and economically threatened who were looking for scapegoats to blame for the nation's woes and for a savior to lead Germany into a brighter future. On hand were Hitler and the Nazis, now being given nationwide publicity by Hugenberg's press, and who, apparently, could offer both.

In the elections of 1930 the party received 18 percent of the national vote and 107 seats in the Reichstag, making them the second-largest party in the parliament after the Social Democrats. In the elections of July 1932 the Nazis won 37 percent of the vote and 230 seats in the Reichstag, still short of a majority but taking over from the Social Democrats as the largest single party. Hitler's road from fringe extremist to national leader was very nearly complete.

2. THE RISE OF FASCIST ITALY

Italy had emerged as one of the victors in World War I, but many in the country felt they had been denied territorial gains that the larger allied powers, Britain and France, had originally promised them. To those on the right who claimed that what the nation had was "a mutilated peace," the ineffectual liberal government of the immediate postwar period was unacceptable, and there was talk of a military coup. In September 1919 the flamboyant playwright and adventurer Gabriele D'Annunzio (1863–1938) led rebellious troops in the occupation of the Adriatic port of Fiume in newly created Yugoslavia. Right-wing nationalists believed that Fiume

The legendary Italian tenor Enrico Caruso at a rally in New York to celebrate the first anniversary of D'Annunzio's occupation of Fiume.

American loans. The withdrawal of this capital produced dramatic effects—wages fell, businesses closed, banks failed, unemployment spread. The comparative prosperity of the period from 1924 to 1929 was seen to be a sham or a will-o'-the-wisp. Early in 1929 unemployment in Germany stood at three million. By September 1931 it was close to 4.5 million, and by the end of 1932 the figure stood at six million. Even those with jobs faced cuts in their income and financial insecurity. There was now a vast army of the unem-

should have been granted to Italy. D'Annunzio's regime there lasted just over a year and inspired no military rising in Italy proper.

MUSSOLINI MAKES HIS APPEARANCE

The two years 1919 and 1920 did, however, see a wave of industrial unrest in Italy, and new parties of left and right emerged. In March 1919 Benito Mussolini (1883–1945) founded a new political movement, the Fascio di Combattimento, and the movement grew rapidly, drawing much of its support from former soldiers disillusioned with the peace. Mussolini was a former socialist and journalist who had come out in support of the war in 1914 and had, indeed, undertaken military service himself. Fascism originally presented itself as a left-wing movement, but it was soon seen as primarily an antisocialist, anti-trade union force. At its heart was an extreme, indeed ferocious nationalism.

Attracting many of the same sort of rootless ex-soldiers who, in Germany, joined the Freikorps, Italian fascism developed a policy of *squadrismo*, violence by fascist squads directed against the parties of the left and against the trade union movement. As this policy was seen more and more in action, Mussolini and the fascists began to receive more and more backing, both moral and financial, from those Italians who felt menaced by socialism and the prospect of an organized working class.

Birth of the Fascist Party

In the elections of May 1921, 35 fascist deputies were elected to the Italian parliament. In November of the same year the movement officially became a political party, the Partito

Nazionale Fascisto. Mussolini, finally abandoning the last pretense to any left-wing credentials, announced a party program that was unashamedly authoritarian and right wing. From now on the PNF was a force in Italian politics that had to be considered, and the traditional ruling parties, both liberal and conservative, sounded out Mussolini and his colleagues about the possibility of fascist collaboration in government.

A portrait of Benito Mussolini in heroic pose. Mussolini's posturing made it difficult for outside observers to take him seriously.

As with Hitler and the Nazis more than a decade later, the political elites assumed that the forces of the radical right could be tamed by inviting them into office. However, the leading Italian fascists had more ambitious ideas about a takeover of power. In October 1922 Mussolini took the

Socialist politician Giacomo Matteotti, shortly before he was murdered in 1924. Mussolini was probably behind the crime.

gerrymandering was opposed by those who still wanted to defend Italian democracy, but they were divided among themselves. The Catholic Partito Popolare decided, after much discussion, to abstain in the vote, and what was known as the Acerbo Bill passed in November 1923.

Matteotti's Murder

The elections of April 1924 were the first under which the new system applied. Fascist intimidation, violence, and corruption reached new levels, but they worked, and the result was an overwhelming victory for Mussolini's party and its allies. When the new, fascist-dominated parliament convened in June, the moderate socialist leader Giacomo Matteotti (1885–1924) launched a blistering and courageous attack on the election,

•

"I, and I alone, assume... responsibility"

•

which he dubbed a fraud, and on the government, which he openly accused of corruption. In doing so Matteotti signed his own death warrant. He disappeared a few days later, and his body was discovered later in the year. He had been kidnapped and murdered, almost certainly on the orders of Mussolini or somebody very close to him.

biggest gamble of his life in planning an insurrectionary march on Rome (see box, opposite). It paid off. Although Luigi Facta, the prime minister, wanted to use the army against the fascists, King Victor Emmanuel III did not and refused to sign a decree of martial law. Facta resigned, and the king called on Mussolini to become prime minister. The March on Rome, instead of an act of potential revolution, became a fascist triumph.

Prime Minister Mussolini

This did not mean that Italy overnight became a fascist country. It had a fascist prime minister in Mussolini, but he presided over a government that was a coalition of a number of political groups. There were very few fascists in the cabinet and still only a small number of fascist

deputies in the parliament. It was not even clear that Mussolini, at this stage, wanted absolute power. For his first two years as prime minister he moved so cautiously that he enraged many of the more radical members of his own party. However, slowly but surely, Italy did move toward dictatorship.

In December 1922 a Fascist Grand Council was established as a channel of communication between the party and the government. It was soon as powerful, if not more so, than the cabinet. In the same month a determined assault on the Communist Party was launched and the arrest of some of its leaders ordered. The following year Mussolini proposed an electoral change whereby the party that performed best in an election would automatically gain two-thirds of the seats in parliament. This blatant attempt at

The March on Rome

In July 1922, powerless in the face of a threat of violence from Mussolini's fascists, Italian prime minister Luigi Facta resigned. He was asked to return to power 12 days later, sparking a socialist-led general strike that was defeated when Mussolini ordered his followers to take over public services.

Mussolini still intended to take power by democratic means but was losing his patience. Now with 200,000 blackshirt followers, he sent fascists to occupy the towns of Bolzano and Trent at the end of September. In October blackshirts began to mass in three armed columns only 30 miles from Rome: 4,000 men at Civitavecchia, 2,000 at Monterotonda, and 8,000 at Tivoli. On October 24 Mussolini addressed 40,000 supporters at the Fascist Party Congress in Naples and announced, "I assure you in all solemnity that the hour has struck. Either they give us the government or we shall take it by marching on Rome. Now it is a matter of days or hours."

While Mussolini traveled to Milan, Facta acknowledged he could not oppose the fascists and resigned, though he would remain in charge until his successor was appointed. On October 28 fascists took over government buildings in numerous towns. The king invited Mussolini to Rome to discuss joining a new government in a senior position. Mussolini insisted that he had to form a government of his own. After trying in vain to find another candidate for the post, the king telegrammed Mussolini with an invitation to do so.

Mussolini, flanked by four of his blackshirt generals, leads a fascist victory parade after his bloodless coup brought him to power in 1922.

There had been no march on Rome. Mussolini traveled to the capital not at the head of an armed column but by train; he said to the stationmaster in Milan, "I want to leave exactly on time. From now on, everything has to function perfectly." He invited his fascist militia to a military review in the city but dispersed them all again before they could cause any trouble. Two weeks later he asked parliament to give him dictatorial powers. By 275 to 90 votes the Chamber of Deputies elected to do so on November 25, 1922. Italy would be in fascist hands for two decades.

On June 12 the opposition deputies withdrew from parliament in what came to be known as the Aventine Secession. Far from forcing Mussolini and the fascists to respect the constitution, this futile gesture merely emphasized the opposition's weakness and divisions. However, the storm over Matteotti's disappearance and the later revelation of his murder, which outraged even some moderate fascists, did throw Mussolini into a panic himself. He would have resigned had the king wanted that, but Victor Emmanuel, unable to see a credible alternative, did not. The fascist radicals now pressed Mussolini to seize the opportunity to eliminate opposition. In January 1925 he did just that. After announcing in the parliamentary chamber that "I, and I alone, assume the political, moral, and historical responsibility for all that has happened," he rid his government of all nonfascist

Pope Pius XI remains highly controversial for his willingness to work with the fascists.

ministers, dismissed the "Aventine" deputies from their seats, and ordered a series of arrests of his enemies. Later in the year an assassination attempt on Mussolini led to the banning of Matteotti's old party, and a further attempt on Mussolini's life was used as an excuse to ban all other political parties in Italy.

However, unlike Hitler in Germany, Mussolini was never able to gain complete totalitarian power and throw off all rivals to his cult. For a start, he ruled with the acquiescence of the monarchy and was never head of state as well as of the government. (In the end, as Italy fell apart during 1943, it was the king who dismissed Mussolini from office.) Again unlike Hitler, Mussolini had significant rivals within his own party, and he expended much political energy in the late 1920s and early 1930s in sidelining troublesome party leaders and replacing them with yes-men like the party secretary Achille Starace.

Fascism and the Church

Most important, the Roman Catholic Church offered a rival ideology that ruled the hearts and minds of millions of Italians. Italy was still a deeply Catholic country, and the pope, with the inherited charisma of his office and his claims to infallibility, was a political as well as a spiritual leader who could not be ignored. This is not to say that Pope Pius XI (1857–1939) was antifascist. A deep social conservative, he valued fascism as a bulwark against the perceived dangers of godless communism. However, he did have misgivings about the social consequences of fascism and its very obvious anticlericalism. He was also eager to advance the Catholic Church's own interests.

Mussolini, himself an atheist and one-time fierce anticleric, was obliged to seek accommodation with the church. The result was the agreement known as the Lateran Pacts, which were signed in February 1929. In these agreements Mussolini recognized the sovereignty of the Vatican City and acknowledged both the independence of the church and its position as the official state religion. He further allowed the social/political organization Catholic Action to remain independent. Despite restrictions placed on it in the next few years, it continued to be the largest such organization outside the control of the Fascist Party.

In return Mussolini expected, and largely got, a degree of moral support from the church. Pius had already compromised his moral independence by staying quiet over the Matteotti affair. There were occasions throughout the 1930s when he spoke out against fascist policies and, particularly, against the racial policies that Mussolini introduced as his regime moved into closer alliance with Nazi Germany. In 1937, in the papal encyclical *Mit Brennender Sorge*, Pius released a clear denunciation of the Nazi regime. However, the church overall, certainly according to its critics, was too often prepared to overlook the brutalities of fascism as long as Mussolini continued to pay lip service to the independence of the papacy.

3. THE STABLE DEMOCRACIES

In the turbulent political atmospheres of Weimar Germany and 1920s Italy extremism of both right and left flourished. In French society there were powerful political and cultural manifestations of extremism, but the republic was strong enough to absorb and neutralize them. There was never in France a party advocating extremist views that looked likely to reach a mass audience. France, although one of the victorious powers in the war, had suffered greatly in terms of loss of manpower and industrial potential. It also emerged from the war with a vast debt.

The first elections after the war, in November 1919, revealed a nation obsessed with a supposed threat from the left, one longing for a return to the certainties of the prewar world. The lower middle class was severely affected by immediate postwar inflation. The parties on the left were divided, and a peculiar system of proportional representation used in this election worked against them. The result was an overwhelming majority for the Bloc National, an

AVEZ VOUS PLACE DANS VOTRE COEUR POUR NOUS?

"Have you room in your heart for us."

Fatherless Children of France. Inc.

"Do you have room in your hearts for us?" is the plaintive plea in this poster published at the end of World War I, as France longed for peace.

alliance of largely right-wing groups who were fervently anticommunist, largely Catholic, and most significantly for the future, determined to make Germany foot the bill for the war. In later elections, in the 1920s, power returned to moderate, center-left republicans and socialists, but France had already been set on the path of determined insistence on German payment of war reparations as specified by the Treaty of Versailles. This was to have large consequences for European diplomacy and the

balance of power on the continent of Europe throughout the 1920s and on into the 1930s.

THE FRENCH CENTER HOLDS

The right in France tended to exercise its power culturally rather than politically. France had a shameful history of anti-Semitism dating back at least as far as the mid-19th century. The Dreyfus affair, in which a Jewish army officer was framed for espionage crimes he did not commit, polarized French society in the years either side of the turn of the century. One of the leading anti-Dreyfusards, the writer and intellectual Charles Maurras (1868–1952), continued his work in the 1920s and 1930s, and the group of people focused around his magazine *Action Française* exercised a cultural influence out of all proportion to its numbers. However, that influence, poisonous though it undoubtedly was, never stretched, or indeed aspired, to any mass following. Extreme right-wing groups remained firmly on the fringes of French politics.

On the far left, although there were major demonstrations and street fighting during this period by leftist groups, the major parties worked within the framework of the republic. In its rhetoric the French Communist Party lambasted parliamentary democracy as a device to keep the workers in their chains. In practice it either slavishly followed the party line established in Moscow or worked within the French political system, often forming electoral alliances with the socialists. At no time did it offer a meaningful threat to the bewildering succession of largely centrist coalition governments that ruled France between the wars.

POSTWAR BRITAIN

In Britain the postwar period brought economic hardship to many and industrial unrest, peaking in the 1926 General Strike, throughout the 1920s and early 1930s. There was, however, despite scaremongering among the right-wing press, little sense of the dangerous extremism that took hold in other European countries. There were strikes in the Glasgow shipbuilding industry on the Clyde River in the immediate postwar years that were often led by the militant left, but "Red Clydeside" was not a forerunner of revolution. The socialist Labour Party took office for the first time in 1924 (briefly) and was again in power between 1929 and 1931, but these governments under prime minister Ramsay MacDonald (1866–1937) were not filled with firebrand revolutionary socialists. In many ways they behaved more cautiously than some of the Conservative administrations of the time.

Even the legendary General Strike of 1926 was not intended to demonstrate the revolutionary potential of the British working class. It originated in the long-

Battle of Cable Street

In October 1936 London's East End became the scene of a street confrontation provoked by Mosley's black-shirted fascists. Antifascists barricaded Cable Street to block a fascist march through the predominantly Jewish area. Police charged the demonstrators, the march was called off to avoid a full-scale battle, and political uniforms were later banned to deprive the blackshirts of their paramilitary appeal.

running disputes between coal miners and the mine owners. In 1925 the Trades Union Congress (TUC) pledged to back the miners by calling sympathy strikes in other industries, if this was required. The following year trouble between miners and owners escalated into a lockout on April 30. The General Strike was called on May 4, but the Conservative government of Stanley Baldwin (1867–1947) had prepared emergency measures, and volunteers, largely middle class, helped run basic services. After a little over a week the TUC abjectly surrendered, and the country returned to normal. The miners, under their leader A. J. Cook, stayed on strike until November but were eventually forced to return to work. If anything, the

A police escort for a volunteer bus driver during the General Strike that gripped Britain in May 1926. The strike lasted little over a week.

General Strike revealed the inadequacies of organized labor and the left in Britain.

Mosley and British Fascism

On the right there were only fringe groups, often cranky and always disorganized, until the advent of Sir Oswald Mosley (1896–1980). Mosley had entered parliament in 1918 as a Conservative and the youngest member of the House of Commons. After a period as an independent member of parliament he joined the Labour Party and, indeed, served in MacDonald's second administration. He resigned in 1931 when his radical ideas about the solution to mass unemployment were ignored. The following year, with unemployment still standing at more than 1.5 million and the Depression still damaging Britain's economy, Mosley founded the New Party and fielded 24 candidates in the general election. All lost heavily. Disillusioned with parliamentary politics and impressed by Mussolini's Italy,

Mosley founded the British Union of Fascists (BUF) in October 1932 and set out on the road that led him to imprisonment in a British jail during World War II.

Although Mosley was a superb orator, and although the BUF attracted a lot of publicity with provocative marches, including one through a predominantly Jewish area of London's East End that ended in a street battle (see box, left, and page 37), the fascists were never a major force in British politics. The economic hardship that drove German people into the arms of the Nazis was not as extreme in Britain, nor was it suffering from that sense of deeply wounded pride that the Treaty of Versailles had inflicted on defeated and demoralized Germany.

4. THE TRIUMPH OF JAPANESE MILITARISM

In Asia, as in Europe, nations were moving toward militarism and the right. Japanese troops had fought against the Germans in World War I, and their seizure of German treaty ports on the

Chinese mainland and German-occupied islands in the Pacific had been among the first successes of 1914 and 1915. Japan participated in the Paris Peace Conference of 1919 and in the early 1920s reached agreements with Britain and the United States about respective spheres of influence in the Pacific (see Volume 1, Chapter 3, "The Return to Normalcy"). On the surface Japan appeared to be moving toward acceptance as one of the great world powers with a significant voice in the postwar reconstruction. Underneath the surface Japan was a society struggling to come to terms with disorienting social change.

The death of Emperor Meiji in 1912 had seen the departure of a symbol of stability and tradition. His successor, by contrast, was mentally ill and, in 1921, had to be replaced by the 20-year-old Prince Hirohito (1901–1989) acting as regent. Inflation struck im-

mediately after the war, and there were riots throughout the country. Industrial unrest, previously a rarity in Japan's hierarchical and deferential society, became commonplace. Economic problems and recession in the early 1920s were compounded by a huge natural disaster—the earthquake of 1923, which virtually destroyed the city of Yokohama and caused severe damage and loss of life (nearly 75,000 dead in Tokyo alone). At the end of the 1920s the Wall Street Crash and the consequent world depression affected Japan as badly as it did other nations, and unemployment rose rapidly.

In these years of change the military seemed to represent stability, and its ties to the people were further strengthened by the creation of patriotic associations in the rural communities, often organized by service veterans, and by the emergence of a number of paramilitary, nationalist, and right-

The aftermath of the earthquake that wrecked the Japanese city of Yokohama in 1923, with great loss of life there and in Tokyo.

wing organizations. Japan was a militarist society both in the sense that military issues were seen to be of major importance in government policy, and in the sense that the influence of the military stretched into all kinds of non-military areas of life.

JAPAN EYES CHINA
As the 1920s went on, voices in the military were increasingly heard calling for the government to prosecute more vigorously Japan's interests in Asia. Most ominously they tended to focus on Japan's policy toward China. To Japan China offered huge economic potential. Japan was a trading nation and needed to export to thrive. China was a potentially vast market. In addition China offered access to a range of raw materials,

The Mukden Incident

In 1915, during World War I, Japan issued the Twenty-One Demands, a series of ultimatums that would leave China as little more than a protectorate of its increasingly potent neighbor. Although the demands were unsuccessful, they clearly announced Japan's aggressive intentions. Japan had already annexed Taiwan in 1895 and Korea in 1910, and in northeastern China had established special rights in Manchuria. The vast province between the Great Wall and the Russian border was the site of a Japanese-owned railroad and mining operations; strategically it protected the colony in Korea and prevented Russian expansion to the north.

In the late 1920s Japanese militarists looked increasingly to Manchuria as a way to acquire land for settlement that would relieve population pressure in Japan. China, however, was becoming increasingly unified by the Nationalist forces of Chiang Kai-shek. Alarmed, the militarists decided to act. On the night of September 18, 1931, Japanese troops stationed in Manchuria used an explosion on the South Manchurian Railroad as a pretext to occupy Manchuria's capital, Mukden.

Japan's Emperor Hirohito and Prime Minister Kijuro Shidehara both condemned the military action, but they were powerless to reverse it. By early 1932 the army had taken all of Manchuria and parts of neighboring Mongolia. Shidehara's government fell. Strong public opinion left its replacement with little realistic option but to support the invasion. The militaristic right wing was firmly in control of Japan.

Chiang Kai-shek, meanwhile, was more concerned with uniting the rest of China than with Manchuria and referred the problem to the League of Nations. When a League commission declared Japan the aggressor in the incident, Japan simply withdrew from the League. In 1935 it used Manchuria as a base from which to advance through northern China, and in 1937 it formally declared war on its neighbor. Japan continued to occupy Manchuria until its defeat at the end of World War II in 1945.

Japanese troops enter Manchuria during their invasion of 1931. The incident signaled that the militarists in Japan were now in charge.

minerals, and so on. Japan was already a colonial power. It governed Taiwan and had annexed Korea in 1910. Conflict with China, particularly over the status of Korea, went back at least as far as the 1880s. To many Japanese on the right, territorial expansion in China seemed only logical.

Japan already had soldiers in Manchuria, part of mainland China, guarding Japanese interests in railways and mines there. On September 18, 1931, a bomb exploded under a Japanese-owned express train in the Manchurian city of Mukden. It was probably planted by Japanese agents, but

Japanese officers in Manchuria, acting without government authorization, used the "Mukden Incident" as an excuse to occupy the territory (see box). The Japanese government was powerless to rein in its military hotheads and in February 1932 accepted the establishment of the puppet state of Manchukuo. The League of Nations condemned Japanese aggression in Manchuria, but Japan responded by leaving the League in 1933. Following a spate of assassinations of leading political figures, including the prime minister in May 1932, the government became increasingly concentrated in the hands of military men. Japan marched on the road that was to lead to Pearl Harbor and a catastrophic war (see Chapter 4, "The Road to War").

THE LEGACY OF WAR

Throughout the 1920s and early 1930s politicians in Europe and Asia had to grapple with the legacies of World War I and the social consequences of economic depression and hardship. In two of the victor nations, Britain and France, democratic institutions were stable enough to survive these consequences. There were pockets of extremism in both societies, but there was never any realistic danger of extremist groups, of either left or right, attaining power.

In a third victor nation, Italy, a less well-established democracy was unable to withstand both the economic shocks of the postwar years and the political opportunism of Mussolini and his Fascist party. In a fourth, Japan, quite different social conditions, fueled by the same worldwide economic crisis, led increasingly to militarism and colonial

Emperor Hirohito, ruler of Japan, was increasingly impotent in the face of militarist politicians.

aggression. In defeated Germany the parliamentary democracy of the Weimar Republic always struggled to sustain itself. Unrealistic demands for war reparations, particularly from France, teamed up with economic depression to plunge the fledgling democracy into a crisis with which it could not cope. Political extremism of right and left had threatened Weimar since its start. When its final hours came, it was, tragically for Germany and the world, Hitler and the Nazi party that were best placed to exploit them.

— SEE ALSO —

◆ Volume 6, Chapter 2, The Victory of Authoritarianism

◆ Volume 6, Chapter 3, Foreign Policy

◆ Volume 6, Chapter 4, The Road to War

◆ Volume 6, Chapter 5, The United States in World War II

The Victory of Authoritarianism in Europe and Asia, 1933–1939

As America recovered from the worst ravages of the Depression, events abroad were changing at breakneck speed. With the aggressive ambitions of Adolf Hitler in Germany the specter of war loomed over Europe. Meanwhile, Japan was emerging as yet another threat.

When Franklin Roosevelt entered the White House in March 1933, questions of foreign policy were not foremost in his mind (see Volume 2, Chapter 2, "The First Hundred Days"). But in both Asia and Europe there were signs of trouble ahead (see Chapter 1, "Economics and Political Extremism"). In 1931 Japan, whose political institutions were looking increasingly fragile against the forces of militarism, had conquered the northern Chinese province of Manchuria. When the League of Nations called for Japan to withdraw its forces and return the province to the Chinese, Japan simply walked out of the League.

In Europe the most alarming development was the installation of the Nazi leader, Adolf Hitler (1889–1945), as chancellor of Germany at the beginning of 1933. The politicians who gave him his chance thought that office would tame him. They miscalculated. Instead, Germany was rapidly transformed into Europe's second fascist state, after Mussolini's Italy, and events were set in train that would lead to war.

1. HITLER TAKES COMMAND

In the German elections held in July 1932 Hitler's National Socialist (Nazi) party had won 37 percent of the popular vote and 230 seats in the Reichstag, or legislature. In doing so it became, for the first time, the largest political party in Germany. There were so many parties represented in the Reichstag, however, that the Nazis did not have a majority.

Swastikas in Berlin (left). Hitler's promise of a new Reich fell on eager ears in a Germany still licking its wounds after World War I.

Hitler's next move was therefore awaited with great interest. On many occasions he had openly voiced his contempt for democracy and his intention to destroy it. How long would the Nazis' patience hold? How many more elections would they have the patience to contest in search of an overall majority?

The question took on added significance when, in the second Reichstag elections of 1932, held in the fall, the number of National Socialist deputies fell by 34. The Nazis depended on a continuing momentum. One of their slogans, used repeatedly, was that Hitler was the "Führer [leader] of the coming Germany." This powerful slogan would lose its force if the feeling that the future inevitably belonged to him was weakened by delay. Some members of the party therefore favored the use of force. Hitler, with memories of the failed putsch of 1923, was more cautious. He decided to bid for the chancellorship.

Throughout the late fall of 1932 and January 1933 negotia-

"Our last hope: Hitler," claims an election poster for the National Socialists. Like America, Germany was on its knees in the early 1930s.

tions went on among the conservative clique at the head of German affairs—the president of the republic, Paul von Hindenburg (1837–1934), and the last two chancellors, Franz von Papen and General Kurt von Schleicher—to discover whether Hitler could be bought off with the vice-chancellorship. He could not, and in the end his defiance won the day. On January 30, 1933, he was sworn in as chancellor. He had not exactly toppled the Weimar republic, because parliamentary democracy already took second place to rule by presidential decree. Had the conservative elements in German politics been loyal defenders of democracy, Hitler might never

The Nazis were relentless propagandists. This poster appeals to women to "save the German family" by voting for Hitler.

Hitler attends a rally in Nurem-berg, Bavaria, 1929. The emotional fervor that attended such events captured Germany's attention.

political inheritance, and a new age had dawned for Germany.

"The man does not really exist—he is only the noise he makes." So, shortly before he came into office, was Hitler summed up by the writer Kurt Tucholsky. It was not an uncommon judgment. Hitler had touched chords deep in many Germans' hearts by his emotional appeals to their wounded national pride and their patriotic yearnings. He had successfully exploited the economic hardships of the people by ranting against what he called the Jewish-capitalist-Marxist conspiracy that was undermining the will of the nation to prosper. But his speeches were empty of details. No one knew what he would do with the responsibility entrusted to him.

THE NAZI REVOLUTION

Many observers, indeed, predicted that the "Bohemian corporal," in the phrase habitually used by Hindenburg to belittle him, would last but a short time in office. He was, after all, a 43-year-old man of no executive experience. Remark-ably, the chancellorship was the

•

"The man does not really exist—he is only the noise he makes"

•

have scaled its walls. As it was, the walls came tumbling down.

The conservatives consoled themselves with the knowledge that Hitler had been placed at the head of a coalition government in which his Nazi Party held a minority of the cabinet posts. They let in the wolf at the gate in the

hope that he would behave with the good manners of an invited guest. "We've hired him for our act," said Papen. But the torchlight procession that hour after hour streamed past the Chancellery in Berlin on the night of January 30 showed something quite different. In the eager faces of the swastika-brandishing fanatics, their arms raised in the Nazi salute as their shouts of "Heil Hitler" broke the crisp winter air, it appeared that a new generation had entered into its

first real job of his life. His Nazi colleagues were greatly out-numbered in the cabinet. And the National Socialist vote had fallen away at the most recent elections to the Reichstag. Hitler came to the chancellorship with the support of only a third of the

Until he turned openly on the Jews, Hitler reserved most of his fury for communists, seen here rallying in Berlin on April 7, 1932.

week in March; but before polling took place, the Nazis received a sensational stroke of luck. On the night of February 27 the Reichstag building went up in flames. As far as can be known, the fire was the work of a young Dutch bricklayer and fanatical anti-Nazi, Marinus van der Lubbe, who was arrested at the scene. But the Nazis had no difficulty in convincing people (Hitler seems to have believed it

German electorate, and he had arrived there not as a revolutionary hero but as the compromise choice of conservative politicians. Yet within 18 months he was to carry the German nation with him in an entire transformation of the political world as he established his dictatorship. He did so while maintaining an extraordinary personal ascendancy in the affections of a majority of Germans.

Hitler represented energy. During the initial stages of his chancellorship that was his most important quality. After years of seeming paralysis, during which governments had come and gone, Hitler, by his youth and his dynamism—and the youth and dynamism of Nazism—embodied the promise of action. The nation's mood was to give him a chance.

The Reichstag Fire

The first opportunity for the nation to express itself came in new elections to the Reichstag. They were scheduled for the first

It was Hitler's good fortune that the Reichstag burned down shortly before the 1933 elections; he falsely accused communists of the arson.

himself) that the fire was the communists' doing, the signal for the outbreak of a "Red revolution." That night thousands of communists were rounded up, mostly in Prussia, and placed in prison: The first of the "concentration camps" for political prisoners was established at an empty munitions factory at Dachau on March 20.

On the morning of February 28 Hitler persuaded President Hindenburg to issue a sweeping emergency decree for the "protection of people and state" against "communist acts of aggression." At a stroke the decree, which had no time limit, dispensed with the civil liberties of the German people. It gave the police unrestricted powers of search, arrest, and detention without trial. It also gave the

"France! Hitler is demolishing the peace." So shouts a poster in Paris, March 1933, voicing deep concern over Hitler's rise to power.

federal government the authority to seize control of provincial police forces. Its immediate consequence was to legalize the reign of terror conducted by the Nazis during the election campaign. Its far-reaching significance was that it was to become the cornerstone of the Nazi dictatorship.

Whipping up anticommunist sentiment (throughout the election campaign Nazi speakers scarcely mentioned the Jews) delivered thousands of votes to the National Socialists. And Hitler's promise to industrialists in February, that this would be the last election so long as he remained in charge of affairs, brought money from big business flowing into the party's coffers. "Give me four years," Hitler said. The electorate's response, despite intimidation and censorship, and despite signs that the economy was beginning to look up, was lukewarm. National Socialist candidates gained 44 percent of the vote, their highest tally ever, but still some way short of a majority.

Man of the Moment

The modest victory, however, proved to be the springboard for Hitler. After those elections there began a mass desertion to the Nazis, not only from the middle classes and the nationalist parties, but also from the Communist Party and its supporters, the Roman Catholic Center Party and the Social Democrats. The graph of Hitler's popular standing turned sharply upward as Germany's political landscape was fundamentally transformed, and the shift in his public image from party leader to national leader began to gain hold.

On March 23 the new Reichstag met in the opera house at Potsdam. As armed Nazi stormtroopers lined the walls, parliament passed an Enabling Act that destroyed the constitution and

•

"It is time for you to decide between peace and war"

•

gave the chancellor (technically, the cabinet) unlimited legislative and executive authority. The act was passed by the astonishing margin of 441 votes to 94. Hitler had ended his speech on the bill with the words, "Now, gentlemen of the Reichstag, it is for you to decide between peace and war," and only the Social Democrats dared to choose war. There were no Communist deputies present, since most of them were in prison, and the rest had gone into hiding. With the passing of the Enabling Act German democracy breathed its last for over 13 years.

Concentration Camps

Concentration camps differ from POW camps and state prisons: They usually serve to house groups of people who are neither detainable under the articles of war nor personally guilty of offenses under state law. Hitler was not the first to use them. After a Cuban revolt in 1895, Spanish troops herded peasants into concentration camps. The British used similar practices against Boer civilians during the South African War of 1901–1902. The corrective labor camps of the Soviet Union, dating from around 1923, were used by Joseph Stalin to dispose of any civilians that he deemed a political threat.

Later in 1933 the Roman Catholic church made its peace with Nazism. By a concordat concluded between Germany and the Vatican, Hitler agreed to protect church property in return for clerical nonintervention in politics. In December the identity of the National Socialist Party and the state was formally decreed in law. Also that month Ernst Röhm (1887–1934), one of Hitler's oldest allies and the head of the SA, the strong-arm brownshirt squads that had played such a conspicuous role in Nazi street politics, was brought into the cabinet. By the summer of 1934 all political parties except the Nazis had been abolished, the trade unions were disbanded, and each of the *länder* (provinces) had been placed under the rule of a Reich governor appointed by Hitler.

Hitler Mania

All this was accomplished with scarcely any outward show of opposition and amid a mounting display of Hitler euphoria. This would suggest that notwithstanding the difficulty in separating staged propaganda from genuine expressions of allegiance, the minority that had voted for National Socialism in March had swelled in a matter of weeks into a large majority. Whatever reservations many people may still have held about the Nazi Party, they went over in their millions to support of the führer. Radio and the press were now exclusively in Nazi control, and the only picture that ordinary people were given of Hitler was the Nazi picture: of "the people's chancellor," as the Nazi newspapers were given to calling him. In July 1934 the greeting "Heil Hitler," increasingly used by ordinary Germans as an everyday mode of address, was

officially termed the "German greeting" and made compulsory for all public employees. The raised and extended right arm of the "Hitler salute" was made obligatory during the singing of the national anthem and of the National Socialist Party song, the "Horst Wessel Lied."

The Night of the Long Knives

Hitler's exalted status was demonstrated by the country's lack of reaction to the purge of the SA, the infamous "Night of the Long Knives," on June 30, 1934. Hitler appears genuinely to have believed evidence given to him by the SS (the Nazi elite corps) and the Gestapo (secret police) that the SA leaders were plotting to overthrow him. In fact, the leaders of the SS and the Gestapo, envious of the SA, fabricated the evidence. Hitler authorized the murder of the SA leaders, including one of his oldest political allies, Ernst Röhm. Doing so helped quell the army's suspicions of the SA's pretensions and radical political

Berlin washerwomen peg freshly laundered Nazi banners out to dry, 1935. By then, Hitler's authority in Germany was absolute.

ideas, and it enabled him to demonstrate that he, the führer, alone dictated events in the country and the pace of change. "In the state there is only one bearer of arms, and that is the army," Hitler told the Reichstag in his speech justifying the murders. "There is only one bearer of the political will, and that is the National Socialist Party."

The purge of the SA took place on one night in towns and cities throughout Germany. The SS also took the opportunity to settle old scores with people quite unconnected with the SA. In total they carried out 83 summary executions. Franz von Papen, who more than anyone had opened the door to the chancellorship for Hitler, had a lucky escape. The bullet intended for him killed his secretary. Yet neither the army nor the Catholic church raised a murmur of protest.

In his defense of his actions before the Reichstag Hitler proudly claimed responsibility for the blood-letting. He gloried in his role as mass-murderer, and he succeeded in convincing the majority of the German people that his ruthlessness had been necessary. By playing on Röhm's homosexuality and high living, he portrayed the savagery as essential to the moral health of the nation.

He also cast himself in the role of preserver of law and order against unruly, conspiratorial elements in the SA. "I was responsible for the fate of the German people, and thereby I became the supreme judge of the German people…I gave the order to shoot the ringleaders in this treason, and I further gave the order to cauterize down to the raw flesh the ulcers of this poisoning of the wells in our domestic life." Perhaps most effectively of all, he stood forth as the champion of the little man, the ordinary German who knew what it was to suffer at the hands of power-inflated petty officials, and who therefore applauded when the führer took action against the "little Hitlers" in his own party.

Hitler recognized that the German people cherished him, not the National Socialist Party. So he felt free to move against the SA, the very soul of the party in its early years. By its silence the nation confirmed his judgment. "You have saved the German people from a great peril," President Hindenburg, now senile and in his final illness, congratulated him by telegram. "He who wishes to make history must also be able to shed blood."

The funeral on August 6, 1934, of Paul von Hindenburg, the Weimar president who had appointed Hitler to chancellor in 1933.

A month later Hitler's unique place in the state, above party, above the law, was confirmed. On August 2, 1934, Hindenburg died. There was no election to find a

•

"He who wishes to make history must also be able to shed blood"

•

successor. By a law issued by the cabinet Hitler assumed the presidency. And the army, the bastion of conservative opinion and the institution most resistant to Hitler mania, swore unconditional obedience, not simply to the president of Germany, but to the führer personally. The "Nazi revolution" was accomplished.

THE GERMAN REVIVAL
In the years between 1933 and 1940 Hitler carried all before him. "I go the way that Providence dictates," he told a cheering Munich crowd in March 1936, just after Germany's military reoccupation of the Rhineland, "with the assurance of a sleepwalker." Five days later, in Hamburg, he flattered his audience by telling it that his strength came from the people. "My pride is that I know no statesman in the world who with greater right than I can say that he is the representative of his people." The statement was true. Germans could hardly believe the astonishing national revival of the mid-1930s. But it took place, and they knew whom to thank for it and in whom to place their trust. The Nazi government gave them peace and prosperity—a series of foreign policy successes and an economic recovery unmatched by any of Germany's industrial rivals.

When Hitler became chancellor, there were six million people unemployed in Germany; by 1937 the total had shrunk to one million. It is often said that this achievement was won by rearmament. That is not the whole

Well-wishers greet German troops during the reoccupation of the Rhineland in 1936, a move that alarmed other European powers.

hundred thousand more. But the recovery was really due to Hitler's perception, which had eluded his predecessors in the chancellery, that the economy needed expansion, not tightening. An ambitious road-building program (the famous autobahns) and the smaller, but important, mass production of radio sets to turn them from luxury items into commonplace household goods were examples of what could be done by government-financed public works and government-backed enterprises. Engineering and automobile production more than doubled their labor forces between 1933 and 1936, while the

story. Military conscription (the draft) removed a few hundred thousand young men from the ranks of the unemployed. The stimulus given to the metal and engineering trades by the expansion of arms and aircraft manufacture added perhaps a few

Crisis in Abyssinia

Alarm at the rearmament of Germany led representatives from France, Italy, and Great Britain to meet at the Italian resort of Stresa in April 1935. The three nations denounced Germany's violation of the Versailles treaty and pledged themselves to defend the peace of Europe. Within six months the so-called "Stresa Front" was in tatters, broken by Italy's invasion of the only independent African nation, Ethiopia, which the Italians called Abyssinia.

Italy already had colonies in northeast Africa—Libya, Eritrea, and Somaliland—and in December 1934 Ethiopian and Italian troops clashed at the oasis town of Walwal. Whether Walwal belonged to Ethiopia or Italian Somaliland was disputed. Italy occupied the town and demanded compensation for the loss of 30 soldiers' lives. The Ethiopian government appealed to the League of Nations, but in October 1935 Italian troops overran the country.

The League of Nations duly branded Italy an aggressor and imposed trade sanctions against it. But the crucial item of oil was left off the sanctions list, and Mussolini was able to defy the League and refuse to withdraw. Great Britain and France did not force the issue, for fear of driving Mussolini into Hitler's arms. The results were disastrous. Mussolini, isolated but not checked, began to court Hitler. In 1937 Italy and Germany allied themselves in the Rome-Berlin axis. More important was the effect of the episode on Hitler. Early in 1936 German troops had reentered the Rhineland, again violating the Versailles treaty. Again, the League and the democracies did not act. Europe's future was transformed. Germany could proceed to build the fortified "Siegfried Line" in the west as a shield for aggressive operations in the east, France was exposed to attack, and Hitler was led to believe that the democracies lacked the will to resist him.

Workers set out to build the new autobahn from Munich to Salzburg in 1934. Massive government funds were poured into road-building.

construction industry saw a quadruple boost in manpower.

All this was achieved, moreover, without inflation and with stable wages. There were other factors in the recovery. Interest-free loans to married women who promised not to take employment took females off the unemployment lists; a "voluntary" labor services scheme amounted to civilian conscription; and the government was able, through its control of the labor unions (with concentration camps lurking in the background for trouble-makers), to peg wages at 1932 levels. Although the government theoretically kept its hands off private property, commerce and industry were tightly regulated by the control of foreign exchanges, state allocation of raw materials to industries, strict controls on investment, and state-administered scarcity of consumer goods to give priority to armaments. Agriculture, too, was organized into a disciplined cartel that

farmers were compelled to join, and that controlled the tenure of land, the trade in agricultural produce, and production methods.

Restored Confidence

For people already at work in 1933 the following five years were not marked by any spectacular rise in the standard of living. What mattered, however, was the mood of confidence and hope that replaced the despair that had settled on the population between 1929 and 1933. Over and over Hitler and his propaganda minister Joseph Goebbels (1897–1945) used the word "miracle" to describe the relationship that had been forged between a führer who was saving the nation and a grateful people.

A NEW NATIONAL SPIRIT

Germany's "economic miracle"— the phrase was not used at the time—was more than a statistical success. Hitler's appeal to young people was always his strongest card, and the idea of miracle was propagated to symbolize the dawn of a bright age to come, a pulling together of men and women of all

classes to work for a future that had only recently seemed closed to them. National Socialism was not simply nationalism; it was also, at least at the level of rhetoric, its own individual brand of socialism. Hitler made the point in an address to trade unionists on May Day, 1933, which that year was also proclaimed National Socialist Day. "The German people," Hitler said, "must learn to know each other again. The millions who have been split up into professions and kept apart by artificial class distinctions, who, foolishly clinging to profession and status, cannot understand each other any longer, must find once more the way to each other." The next day the independent labor union organization was suppressed. Yet three years later foreign statesmen like David Lloyd George, the former British prime minister, were applauding Hitler on his success.

Grudging acknowledgment of Hitler's achievements, which ate away at opposition to him, was made easier by the fact that the worst fears of 1933 had not come to pass. Hitler had vowed that "heads would roll." But the "November criminals"—the politicians he had blamed for Germany's surrender in 1918 and the subsequent humiliation of Versailles—had merely been interned and, most of them, subsequently released. The terror that had raged on the streets in 1933 and early 1934 decreased after the Röhm purge. And the Olympic Games of 1936, held at Berlin, brought the regime considerable prestige. They became Nazi Germany's showcase to the world (thousands of doves were released at the opening ceremony to show Hitler to the world as a man of peace). From its peak of

The Night of Broken Glass

Only weeks after coming to office Hitler began a campaign against Germany's Jews. On April 7, 1933, members of the professions and public servants "not of Ayran descent," that is, people who were one-quarter or more Jewish, lost their jobs. After the Nuremberg Laws in September 1935 no Jew could be a German citizen. Jews lost the right to vote, and Germans were forbidden to marry or date Jews. Existing "mixed marriages" were dissolved.

The German people made little protest until the pogrom of November 9–10, known as *Kristallnacht*, "the night of broken glass." After a German official was killed by a Jew, Joseph Goebbels, the Nazi propaganda minister, ordered the SA and the SS to unleash violence against Jews throughout the Reich. Over the next 24 hours 100 Jews were killed, hundreds wounded, and more than 30,000 sent to concentration camps. Some 7,500 Jewish businesses and 250 synagogues were destroyed.

Hitler was taken aback by the silence with which the pogrom was received by most Germans. The unexpected reaction convinced the Nazi leadership that plans for the "Final Solution," the extermination of the Jewish population, would have to be devised and carried out in secret.

The smashed window of a Jewish store in Berlin on November 10, 1938, the morning after Kristallnacht.

nearly 27,000 in the summer of 1933 the total of political prisoners fell to about 7,500 in 1937, after which the numbers began to rise once more. The number was never small, but much worse had been expected.

In government Hitler did, of course, behave in accordance with the venom that he had poured on the Jewish people in his speeches before 1933. The Nuremberg Laws of 1935 deprived Germany's Jews of basic civil rights. But, apart from a one-day boycott of Jewish shops a few weeks after Hitler's coming into office, the German people were able to pretend not to see the anti-Semitism of the government until the outright attack on shops and synagogues on Kristallnacht in November 1938. There were, in short, grounds for Germans and outside observers to tell themselves that Hitler was not, on the evidence, the incarnation of evil that his enemies had painted him.

2. HITLER ON THE INTERNATIONAL STAGE

Economic recovery was accompanied by a string of successes in foreign policy. Rearmament, which turned Germany from a nation of 100,000 soldiers without modern weapons and without an air force into the strongest military and air power by 1938, was a triumph of foreign policy and a slap in the face to Great Britain and France. Rearmament breached the Versailles treaty, removing a stigma on the national honor and regaining for Germans what they believed to be their country's rightful place in international diplomacy and politics.

Success home and abroad

Hitler brought off one coup after another in the foreign field with barely a hint of national resistance

Hitler admires the engine of the Volkswagen, or "people's car," in April 1938. At left is the new car's designer, Ferdinand Porsche.

and, so it appeared, without the risk of war. The introduction of general conscription in 1935—celebrated with an awe-inspiring parade to mark the rebirth of the Reichswehr (the German armed forces)—and the remilitarization of the Rhineland in 1936; the absorption into the Reich (the German nation) of Austria and the Sudetenland in 1938: It seemed there was nothing that the führer could not do, no feat of which he was not capable, no goal to which his will would not carry him.

Those triumphs in the foreign field had a further consequence of great importance. They diverted attention from domestic grumbles—full employment did not prevent occasional severe food shortages, for example—and enabled Hitler to whip up enthusiasm just when it was lagging. The Rhineland was occupied for strategic and diplomatic purposes, but the timing, in March 1936, owed much to the fact that for some months the Nazi leadership had

been concerned about ebbing morale in the country.

Against a background of order and stability, coups such as the march into the Rhineland and the *Anschluss* ("union") with Austria sustained Hitler in the popular imagination as the inspired leader of a dynamic nation on the move.

A Reply to Roosevelt
On April 28, 1939, Hitler gave his own assessment of his achievement in a speech to the Reichstag, in which he also denounced the German-Polish Nonaggression Treaty of 1934. The closing passage was a scornful response to a request from Franklin D. Roosevelt. The American president had asked Hitler and the Italian dictator, Benito Mussolini (1883–1945), to pledge themselves to 10

years of nonaggression against other countries (see Chapter 3, "Foreign Policy").

"Mr. Roosevelt! I fully understand that the vastness of your nation and the immense wealth of your country allow you to feel responsible for the history of the whole world and for the history of all nations. I, sir, am placed in a much more modest and smaller sphere.... I cannot feel myself responsible for the fate of the world, as this world took no interest in the pitiful state of my own people...

"I have overcome chaos in Germany, restored order, enormously raised production in all fields of our national economy.... I have succeeded in completely resettling in useful production those seven million unemployed who so touched all our hearts.... I have not only politically united the German nation, but also rearmed it militarily, and I have further tried to liquidate that treaty sheet by sheet whose 448 articles contain the vilest rape to which nations and human beings have ever been expected to submit. I have restored to the Reich the provinces grabbed from us in 1919; I have led millions of deeply unhappy Germans, who had been snatched away from us, back into the fatherland; I have restored the thousand-year-old historical unity of German living space; and I have endeavored to attain all this without spilling blood and without bringing to my people, and consequently to others, the misery of war."

From the day that Hitler took office in January 1933 down to the beginning of 1938, he preached the gospel of peace. He regained the Rhineland, he took Germany out of the League of Nations, he rebuilt the army; and in doing those things he restored Germany to its place among the world's great powers. All that he did without shedding blood and without committing German arms to action. In speech after speech he proclaimed himself to be a man of peace. All the time, however, he had war in his sights. His vision went far beyond the mere creation of a Greater Germany that should incorporate Austria—the dream of many a German nationalist since the mid-19th century—for he meant to bring into existence a vast German empire, extending throughout eastern Europe and absorbing even the Soviet Union.

Hitler's aggressive designs were kept secret (though the scheme was envisioned in *Mein Kampf*, the autobiography that he wrote in prison in 1923–1924), not simply because it was prudent to keep foreign governments in the dark, but because it was essential to deceive the German people.

Fifteen thousand Americans march down New York's Eighth Avenue in 1935 to protest against the rise of Hitler's Nazi Party.

Hitler knew that they were not ready for war. They applauded his diplomatic triumphs. Flouting the Versailles Treaty stirred their patriotism. But the generation of the 1930s, those men and women who had lived through the horrors of World War I, was not in the mood to make sacrifices. Alongside the blossoming of the Hitler cult in the mid-1930s, therefore, ran an undercurrent of nervous apprehension, of alarm that Hitler might one day go too far and at last provoke the democracies into resistance.

The Gloves Come Off

In late 1937 and early 1938 there was a discernible shift in Hitler's mood, a growing sense of urgency. Always fearful that he had not long to live, and convinced that he alone possessed the energy and will needed to build a lasting German empire, he began to lose patience with being merely the leader of a national revival. He decided to move quickly toward

Hitler's Hidden Plans for War

As Hitler confided to newspaper editors at a private meeting in November 1938, it had been necessary for him to pose as a man of peace; but it was also necessary, before the German spirit became weakened by easeful prosperity, to end the years of dissembling.

"Circumstances compelled me to speak of almost nothing but peace for years on end. Only by continually emphasizing Germany's wish for peace and its peaceful intentions was I able to give the German people...the rearmament that was necessary, time and again, as a prerequisite of the next step. It is obvious that such peace propaganda, conducted year after year, also has its difficult side; it can too easily result in the idea taking root in the minds of many people that the present regime as such identifies itself with the resolution and will to preserve peace under all circumstances. But that would lead not only to a wrong assessment of the goals of this system, above all, it would lead to a situation in which the German nation was imbued with a spirit which, in the long run, would become defeatism and would liquidate, and be bound to liquidate, the very success of the present regime."

Nazis march into Salzburg, March 1938. Having annexed Austria, Hitler moved swiftly on to dismember Czechoslovakia.

war, to risk all for the sake of a greater objective: German mastery in Europe, the ascendancy of the Aryan race, and the establishment of a thousand-year Reich.

National Socialism and war, that was to say, were inseparable. Hitler was compelled to embark on an aggressive course of action. It may appear that to do so was to place his achievements at risk, but in his eyes the risk lay in not doing so. What could not be known was how far the German people were prepared to follow him.

The first step was to secure Greater Germany, the union of Germany and Austria; the second was to absorb the so-called "Sudetenland" of Czechoslovakia, the preponderantly German-speaking provinces of Bohemia and Moravia. There is little doubt that at the beginning of 1938 Hitler had no clear idea how to achieve those objectives. He expected to gain Austria without war and, indeed, as it turned out,

the Anschluss and the acquisition of the Sudetenland marked, really, the last phase—even though they were Hitler's first annexations of foreign territory—of the years of peaceful achievement. Neither victory was won without a show of force, but each was won without recourse to arms and without the armed intervention of foreign powers. Between the two there was, of course, a great difference. The Austrian crisis in the late winter and early spring of 1938 did not overtly signal a new reckless policy. The Munich crisis of the autumn (see box, page 40), from which Hitler emerged with the Sudetenland, was a prelude to war.

Anschluss with Austria

The road to the Anschluss was paved by the underground Nazi movement in Austria, which, encouraged and funded from Berlin, brought terror to the nation's streets. Its propaganda focused on high unemployment and exposed the raw nerve of Austria's diminished status as a country after 1918—a pale shadow of the former Austro-Hungarian empire. It urged

Austrians to look to Hitler as a savior, to call on him to do for Austria what he had done for Germany. The Austrian chancellor, Kurt von Schussnigg, knew that the ground was sinking beneath his feet. His appeals to the democracies, especially Great Britain, and to Italy to guarantee Austria's independence were not answered.

On February 12, 1938, he was summoned to the Berghof and treated to an outburst from Hitler. Secure in the knowledge that Austria was internationally isolated, Hitler informed Schussnigg that the history of Austria had been one long, continuous "betrayal of the people." The "historical contradiction" that Austria represented had "come to its long overdue end." Hitler warned Schussnigg that he was determined to put an end to all of it. "You certainly are not going to believe that you can delay me by so much as half an hour. Who knows, perhaps I'll suddenly turn up in Vienna overnight, like the spring storm. Then you'll see something." Powerless to resist, Schussnigg signed the "Berghof agreement." It gave Austrian Nazis the freedom to agitate within the law, made Austrian foreign and economic policy subservient to that of the Reich, and placed in the office of Austrian minister for security and the interior Hitler's "poodle," Arthur Seyss-Inquart.

Whether Hitler would have been content to build gradually on the foundations laid by that agreement cannot be known. Schussnigg brought matters to a head on March 8 by making a "dash for freedom." He announced that a national plebiscite would be held five days later to ask the Austrian people whether they wished Austria to be united with

Fascism beyond Germany and Italy

The roots of fascism lay not in Hitler's Nazi Party but in the ideas of French and, more importantly, Italian political theorists in the years immediately following World War I. With Mussolini's rise to power, and with the added impetus from Germany, fascist movements had by the mid-1930s found fertile soil in many parts of Europe and also the United States.

Wounded national pride, accompanied by postwar depression and whetted by poverty and unemployment, was frequently a catalyst for the violent political upheaval that featured in many fascist uprisings. So, too, were racism and religious fundamentalism. In Romania the Legion of the Archangel Michael (later the Iron Guard) campaigned for Christianization and racial cleansing, with Jews the chief scapegoats. Greek fascists sought to create a "third Hellenic nation."

In Hungary and Poland, as in Romania, hatred toward Jews was integral to fascism. The Hungarian government legislated against Jews in the 1920s, while greenshirt fascists marched the streets brandishing their cross and arrow symbol. Poland experienced anti-Semitism in the troubled years following World War I. And after the death of dictatorial leader Jozef Pilsudski in 1935, who had done much to suppress violence against Jews, the country once again slid toward an anti-Semitic stance.

Sir Oswald Mosley, leader of the British Union of Fascists, addresses a rally in 1935.

Civil war in Spain in 1936–1939 led to the fascist rule of General Francisco Franco, who considered himself answerable "only to God and to History." A vocal agent of fascism in Europe was the British politician Oswald Mosley. Impressed by Hitler, he abandoned traditional political process to pursue a more radical path through fascist agitation.

In the U.S. Nazi sympathizers and anti-Semites joined the German-American Bund. A paramilitary organization, covertly assisted and funded by Nazi Germany in the years before America's entry into World War II, it set up training camps throughout the U.S. By 1939 its membership stood at around 20,000. Smaller extremist cells included the Carolina-based Silver Shirts and the Christian Front.

A car sticker of 1940 reads "Member Ger-Am Bund. Heil Hitler!" By then, with the U.S. at the brink of war, the Bund was close to crumbling.

The Spanish Civil War

At the end of the 1930s Spain became the third democracy in Western Europe to succumb to fascism. After a civil war that lasted from July 1936 to April 1939, General Francisco Franco, the head of the fascist movement called the Falange, became the dictator of Spain.

The civil war was only incidentally a struggle between fascism and communism. The main players on the Nationalist right, though they included the fascists, were the military and the monarchists, strongly backed by the Roman Catholic Church. Nor was the Republican left primarily communist. Just as significant were the social democrats and the anarchists. However, communist participation was powerful enough to help deter the governments of the Western democracies from coming to the aid of Spanish democracy. Germany, Italy, and the Soviet Union, although each of those countries signed a non-intervention agreement at the beginning of the war, entered the fray. Before Christmas of 1936 Mussolini was supplying rifles, machine-guns, and troops (60,000 by the end of 1937) to the Nationalists. Hitler also provided war material and used the conflict to give his air force a workout. The Soviets sent aircraft, tanks, and ammunition—at great cost to their gold and silver reserves.

Foreign intervention was not decisive in determining the outcome of the war. But the conflict, which cost a million lives, was a foretaste of "total war"—especially evident when German planes bombed the civilian population of the Basque town of Guernica. And the heightening of the ideological battle between right and left convinced many observers that they were witnessing a "dress rehearsal" for World War II.

Spanish soldiers give the fascist salute during the brutal civil war, 1937. The Nationalist rebels comprised various extremist factions.

The Bersaglieri, crack troops of Mussolini's army, fighting in the Spanish Civil War. Il Duce, like Hitler, supported the rebels.

Germany. His intention was to demonstrate to the world that Hitler's boast that he commanded the support of the majority of the Austrian people was hollow. The world never found out. Hitler vacillated, but Hermann Göring, the minister of aviation, insisted on mobilization against Austria. He had been assured by Joachim von Ribbentrop, the German ambassador to Great Britain who had just been appointed foreign minister, that Great Britain (and therefore France also) would not interfere. On March 11—the day before the plebiscite was due to take place—Hitler demanded the resignation of Schussnigg and his replacement by Seyss-Inquart. When German divisions streamed into Vienna, Schussnigg announced his resignation on the radio and instructed the Austrian army to offer no resistance.

On the following afternoon Hitler himself crossed into Austria at the border town of Braunau, his birthplace. He then made a four-hour progress, along roads lined at places with cheering crowds and festooned with spring flowers, to Linz. The tumultuous reception that he received determined him to annex Austria then and there. That night he signed a law that proclaimed the "reunion" of Austria with the German Reich. The next day he presented himself to the people of Vienna on the balcony of the Hofburg, the Habsburgs' imperial palace at the heart of the city. While thousands of jubilant Viennese cheered and waved in the Heldenplatz in front of the palace, Hitler reported to history, as he grandly put it, "the entrance of my homeland into the German Reich."

The Fall of Czechoslovakia

The Anschluss was the pinnacle of Hitler's career. The German people's initial anxiety, caused by mobilization and invasion, gave way to joyful relief when it became apparent that Hitler had gotten away with it. Once again the führer appeared able to bring off whatever he wished. In the spring of 1938 Hitler's popularity and prestige were at their peak. The German nation now had everything it asked for. Not, however, Hitler. Two weeks later he met Konrad Henlein, the leader of the Sudeten Germans of Czechoslovakia, and told him that the Czechoslovakian "question" would be solved in the near future. He had resolved, as he put it in a directive to the German General Staff on May 30, to "smash Czechoslovakia by military action."

That approach was not necessary. It had been made clear during meetings in April that neither Great Britain nor France would attempt to restrain Hitler, since their intervention would be read as an attempt to curtail the Sudeten Germans' right to self-determination. As the year wore on, Hitler railed against what he called the "artificial" state of Czechoslovakia. Meanwhile, his armed forces prepared to invade. By September the British prime minister, Neville Chamberlain, and the French premier, Edouard Daladier, were drawing up plans by which predominantly German-speaking parts of Sudetenland might be ceded to the Reich. The Czechoslovak government balked at the proposal, but its hands were tied: The Western powers would not support any measure that would provoke Hitler's rage. A flurry of meetings concluded on the 29th at Munich, where Chamberlain, Mussolini, and Daladier effectively handed the Sudetenland to Hitler in return for a promise of good behavior (see box, page 40). It was the beginning of the end for Czechoslovakia, and in March 1939 German troops entered Prague. Hitler then set his sights on Poland.

As early as 1935 Hitler had preached neutrality with Poland, denying any intention to carve it up with the Soviets to the east. But

The Munich Agreement

By taking over Austria at the point of a gun in March 1938, Hitler had for the first time acted aggressively outside German territory in open defiance of the Treaty of Versailles of 1919. The muted reaction of Britain and France to his action emboldened him further. The nation of Czechoslovakia, created out of the old Austro-Hungarian empire at the end of World War I, was now surrounded on three sides by the expanded Reich. Within its frontiers Czechoslovakia contained about three million Germans, most of them living near the German border in the Sudetenland.

There was much support for the Nazis among Sudetenland Germans, and Hitler's increasingly strident demands that the Sudetenland be ceded to the Reich fell on receptive ears. However, unlike the case with Austria, which had no defensive alliances, Czechoslovakia had a firm treaty with France, and a strong Czech army was prepared to defend itself against mighty Germany.

France and its ally Britain were terrified of a European war breaking out over the Czech question. British prime minister Neville Chamberlain flew three times to Germany in September 1938 to try to negotiate some sort of a settlement with Hitler. Chamberlain believed in a policy of appeasement, by which was meant conciliating Hitler in the belief that if he got what he wanted through negotiation, he would have no cause to resort to force. Such a policy, of course, was based on the assumption that there were limits to Hitler's demands. But Chamberlain, like all Europeans who had lived through World War I only 20 years before, had a mortal dread of any repeat of that calamity

and felt justified in going to almost any lengths to avert it.

On his third and final visit to Hitler, on September 29, the two were joined in Munich by Premier Daladier of France and the Italian dictator and Hitler ally Mussolini (two Czech diplomats at the summit were excluded from the discussions). The world held its breath as the issue of war or peace was debated. A face-saving formula was agreed by which the Sudetenland would be ceded to the Germans and Czechoslovakia's shrunken frontiers guaranteed by all signatories. Chamberlain returned home and at the airport waved the signed agreement to a cheering throng, declaring that the Munich agreement meant "peace for our time...peace with honor." Six months later his boast rang hollow when German troops entered Prague. The Munich sellout, which was never forgotten by the Czechs, utterly discredited the policy of appeasement.

Hitler flanked by Mussolini and his own interpreter, with Chamberlain on the right. The Munich deal was another victory for Hitler.

The Great Wall is no obstacle to Japanese troops as they march through Shanshi Province in northern China, November 1937.

that is what he did. After the annexation of Czechoslovakia, Hitler gradually courted the USSR. The world was stunned by the signing, on August 23–24, of a German-Soviet nonaggression pact. The handshake left no doubt in anyone's mind that Hitler had designs not only on Poland but on the rest of Europe, too. On August 31 Hitler announced hostilities against Poland. Three days later, on September 3, Great Britain and France declared war on Germany.

3. JAPANESE MILITARISM

In the Far East war was already raging. Japan's seizure of theManchurian capital of Mukden from China in 1931 (see box, page 22) marked the beginning of the army's ascendancy in Japanese politics. When the Japanese government, which had been kept in the dark about the army's intentions, accepted a League of Nations resolution calling for a withdrawal, the army simply ignored the government. By the beginning of 1932 it had conquered the whole of Manchuria, renamed it Manchukuo, and set up a puppet Chinese government there under the last Chinese emperor before the establishment of a republic in 1911, Pu Yi. For a second time the League of Nations called on Japan to restore China to its rightful place in Manchuria. In response, Japan quit the League.

Early in 1932 the Japanese prime minister, Tsuyoshi Inukai, who had tried in vain to curb the rising power of the military in Japanese politics, was assassinated

by naval officers. Inukai was the last prime minister to attempt to govern Japan independently of the army. It was a symptom of the growing spirit of militarism in many reaches of Japanese society that Inukai's murderers, who behaved throughout their trial as national heroes, escaped capital punishment. In the new government the most powerful voice belonged to the ultra-nationalist war minister, Sadao Araki (1877–1966). Japan had entered what its historians have

called the *kurai tamina*, or "dark valley," a period marked by political repression and censorship of democratic groups at home and sustained aggression abroad.

For the rest of the decade there was little check on the ambitions of the Japanese army. Little by little, northern China was conquered, until by 1935 a vast area extending from the Great Wall to the outskirts of Beijing (Peking) was under Japanese occupation. No foreign country came to China's assistance. The United States,

A Chinese boy waves a Japanese flag as his homeland is invaded in 1937. Japan relinquished its hold on northern China in 1945.

announced in 1934 that it no longer considered itself bound by the Washington Treaty of 1922, which had imposed limits on the size of the Japanese navy. At the beginning of the 1930s Japan had one aircraft carrier; by 1941 it had 10 (the U.S. Navy had only seven, of which three were in the Pacific). The elegant, swift Fubuki-class destroyers became known as "wolves of the sea." More awesome were the four battleships built secretly after 1937, including the *Yamato* and the *Musashi*, which at that time were the largest battleships ever built.

The purpose of Japan's naval expansion was unmistakable. Japan coveted the raw materials of its neighbors in the Far East—the Philippines, Malaya, Indochina, and the Dutch East Indies (now Indonesia)—to maintain its program of industrialization and to support its rapidly expanding population. Those four countries were under the control, respectively, of the United States, Great Britain, France, and the Netherlands. Japanese leaders proclaimed that they would lift the yoke of Western imperialism from the region and lead it toward a "new order," to which they gave the grand name the "Greater East Asia Co-Prosperity Sphere." Before making its military bid in the Pacific, Japan needed to end its diplomatic isolation. That was accomplished in November 1936 by the signing of the Anti-Comintern pact with Nazi Germany. The pact had the flimsy purpose of committing both nations to opposition to international communism. By it, however, Japan

which alone was powerful enough among the western democracies to defend China, was still in the isolationist mood that had prevailed since the end of World War 1, when it had refused to join the League of Nations (see Volume 1, Chapter 3, "The Return to Normalcy"). American policy in the 1930s was to disengage itself from commitments in the Pacific. In 1934 Congress voted to relinquish its military bases in the Philippines, and the Pentagon allowed the island base of Guam to decline into a state of neglect.

The New Japanese Navy

Japan, by contrast, embarked on a program of naval expansion. Japan had emerged as a world naval power in 1905, when its navy won a crushing victory over the Russian fleet at the Battle of Tsushima. But its ships then, and for two decades and more afterward, were largely British-built. In the 1930s Japan broke the link with the British shipyards and decided to build a navy for itself capable of exercising mastery in the Pacific. In order to have a free hand, the government also gained German recognition for its occupation of Manchuria and, by implication, German support for any further Japanese aggression against China.

War in the East

In 1935 the Italian invasion and conquest of Abyssinia (Ethiopia) had led Hitler, impressed by the failure of the League of the Nations or the western democ-racies to halt Mussolini, to contemplate a pact with Italy. The Rome-Berlin axis was ratified in 1937, adding a European fascist alliance to the Asian axis. Having linked its future with European fascism, Japan unloosed its army on Peking in July 1937. Within a year Japanese troops controlled most of China's coastline, major cities, and railways. World War II in the East had begun.

A great pall of smoke billows over North Shanghai, its Chinese inhabitants fleeing shortly before Japanese troops encircle the city.

The Imperial Way Faction

Among the many extremist right-wing societies that flourished in Japan during the interwar years the most influential was the Imperial Way Faction. Its leading intellectual light, Ikki Kita, published a book called *A Plan for the Reorganization of Japan* in 1923, the year of Hitler's abortive Munich putsch.

Like Mussolini and Hitler, Kita fused aggressive nationalism with egalitarian socialism. As in Italy and Germany the nationalism was by far the more important ingredient. Kita called for a coup d'état to overthrow Japanese parliamentary institutions and install a "revolutionary empire of Japan," in which emperor and army should lead the country in its destiny to rule over an Asian empire that would include China and India. Only Japan could rid Asia of western imperialists, especially Great Britain, "a multimillionaire standing over the whole world."

Kita's ideas found a receptive ear in the army, especially in the person of General Sadao Araki, who was appointed minister of war in 1931 and as such was the principal instigator of Japanese aggression against China. By offering the people social equality—all property owned by the princes of industry, the *zaibatsu*, was to be surrendered to the emperor—combined with the promise of Asian liberation and imperial glory, the radical right gained a mass following. Parliamentary institutions were never abolished in Japan, but as the 1930s went on, the political parties found themselves powerless to prevent the army from becoming the arbiter of the nation's affairs.

3

ROOSEVELT'S FOREIGN POLICY, 1933–1939

When he assumed office, President Roosevelt made it abundantly clear that his priority was the domestic crisis facing the U.S., not foreign affairs. However, as war clouds gathered over Europe and East Asia during the 1930s, it became increasingly difficult—and eventually impossible—for Americans to stand on the sidelines as the world moved inexorably toward conflict.

When Franklin D. Roosevelt entered the White House in March 1933, the United States was nearly four years into a deepening depression (see Volume 2, Chapter 2, "The First Hundred Days"). Its banking system was on the verge of collapse. The morale of the people was at a low ebb. As he began to grapple with the acute domestic crisis, almost the last thing on the president's mind was the country's relations with the rest of the world. His inauguration speech contained only one fleeting reference to the outside world, and that was no more than a bland expression of sentiment. The United States, he said, was dedicated to playing the role of a "Good Neighbor."

Not until his annual message to Congress in January 1936 did Roosevelt speak at length to the American people on issues of foreign policy. And he then did so

President Roosevelt in 1937 unwittingly makes what will become the Allies' V for victory gesture during World War II.

in order to reassure them of his resolve amid rising international tensions in Europe to preserve American neutrality and keep the nation out of war (see Chapter 2, "The Victory of Authoritarianism in Europe and Asia"). Down to the outbreak of World War II in September 1939 that remained Roosevelt's public position (see Chapter 4, "The Road to War").

Historians have been divided in their assessment of Roosevelt's foreign policy. Some have argued that FDR was an internationalist at heart who, against his instincts, decided not to buck the isolationist mood of the 1930s for fear of alienating the people and thus putting at risk his program for economic recovery. That interpretation has led to the charge that he failed to provide leadership in foreign affairs. Other historians have found in Roosevelt's public and private statements evidence that he was himself an isolationist, and that his essentially do-nothing foreign policy before the outbreak of World War II was a true reflection of his own beliefs, not a recourse to political expediency. One

A meeting of the League of Nations Council in London in 1935. Without American participation the League proved an ineffective peacekeeper.

fundamental matter seems, at least, to be beyond controversy. In sticking to a policy of isolationism, there is no doubt that Roosevelt acted in tune with the instincts and wishes of the great majority of the American people.

1. THE POLICY OF ISOLATIONISM

Ever since President Washington, in his farewell address in 1796, had warned the American people not to allow their government to involve them in "foreign entanglements," they had been reluctant participants in overseas affairs. In 1920 the Senate had declined to ratify American membership in the League of Nations, and during the 1932 election campaign Roosevelt dismayed internationalists by announcing that he was opposed to American entry into the organization. The statement received the warm approval of arch-isolationists like Senator

Movie star Gary Cooper reading Ernest Hemingway's novel A Farewell to Arms *on the set of the movie based on the story, in 1932.*

William Borah of Idaho, who was later to describe the League as "nothing more than a cog in the military machine of Europe."

Historically, the United States had, since winning its independence, played little part in the international power politics of the Old World. Having reluctantly entered World War I nearly three years after it had begun (see Volume 1, Chapter 2, "The United States in World War I"), Americans were wary of becoming embroiled once more in the quarrels beyond their borders. That isolationist mood was reflected in the writings of prominent Americans. Charles Beard (1874–1948), a controversial but esteemed historian, wrote a number of books and essays in the 1930s that popularized the view that America's role was to restrict itself to exercising peaceful leadership and promoting democracy in the Western Hemisphere. Ernest Hemingway's best-

Recognizing the Soviet Union

One of the by-products of the Great Depression was that the United States, more than a decade after the Bolshevik triumph in the Russian civil war, at last accorded the government of the Soviet Union official recognition. There were many Americans, especially in the labor union movement, who wanted to have nothing to do with the Soviet Communist regime. Church leaders, too, expressed concern about seeming to give an American blessing to Marxism.

At the same time, a number of leaders in the business sector, men such as James Mooney, the vice-president of General Motors, and Thomas Morgan, the head of Curtiss-Wright and Sperry Gyroscope, pressed on the White House the argument that recognition would boost trade with the USSR, which was the world's largest importer of American industrial goods and agricultural machinery.

Soviet diplomat Maxim Litvinov after gaining the USSR's admission to the League of Nations in 1934, a year after achieving U.S. recognition.

The Soviet foreign minister, Maxim Litvinov (1876–1951), was invited to meet President Roosevelt in order to negotiate the terms of American recognition. He arrived at Union Station, Washington, on November 7, 1933, and was greeted by state department officials—none of them wearing the top hat that was customary for top-level diplomatic meetings because Litvinov did not represent a recognized government. Outstanding Soviet war debts on loans from the U.S. Treasury and private individuals were expected to be a sticking point, but after nine days of negotiations it was agreed to defer the settlement of those debts—somewhere between $75 and $150 million—to a later date. The Soviet Union promised to guarantee the freedom of religious worship for Americans resident in the USSR and not to support the American Communist Party.

Recognition was granted in a formal exchange of documents on November 16. The Soviet Union, however, reneged on its pledges. Moscow invited American Communists to attend the Congress of the Third International in 1935 and refused to settle the debt issue. Trade between the countries declined. But Roosevelt had done nothing more than recognize the fact of Communist rule. He had opened channels of communication between Washington and Moscow that were to be important during World War II.

selling novel *A Farewell to Arms*, set in World War I and published in 1929, was a powerful depiction of the futility of war.

From the very beginning of his presidency Roosevelt signaled that he had little interest in cooperating with the European powers in their attempts to arrest the growth of rearmament or to find international solutions to the economic depression that held the world in its grip. He came into office when the Geneva disarmament conference was in session. America sent a delegation to the conference, and Roosevelt himself declared that disarmament was crucial to world peace. He even proposed a reduction in the size of the U.S. Army. But despite alarms that the new chancellor of Germany, Adolf Hitler (1889–1945), meant to override the Treaty of Versailles and reestablish Germany as a military power, Roosevelt refused to give the conference the backing and commitment from the United States that was essential to any credible program of disarmament.

The French government wanted a guarantee that the United States would resist German aggression. Given the American mood, the French government was being unrealistic. The most that Roosevelt did was to allow one of his special representatives, Norman Davis, to announce that if the League of Nations were to decide to apply sanctions against Germany, the United States would not interfere with such sanctions. Germany withdrew from the disarmament conference and, a few months later, from the League of Nations itself. Roosevelt has been much criticized for his apparent indifference to Nazi aggression, but there is no reason to suppose that a stronger line from the White House would have deterred Hitler from carrying out his program of German rearmament.

FAILURE TO FIND ECONOMIC AGREEMENT

Roosevelt also adopted a cautious attitude toward the London Economic Conference that convened in June 1933. The purpose of the conference was to discuss ways in which the nations of the world could cooperate to overcome the Great Depression. Outwardly, Roosevelt seemed to welcome the conference, but his actions belied his words. The roaring inflation that had hit a number of countries in the 1920s had been exploited by right-wing parties and contributed to the rise of fascism and its German variant Nazism in Europe (see Chapter 1, "Economics and Political Extremism"). One of the aims of the organizers of the London Economic Conference was, therefore, to seek ways to achieve worldwide monetary

stability. But two months before the conference opened, Roosevelt dealt a blow to European hopes by announcing that the United States, like Great Britain in 1931, was coming off the international gold standard. That meant that the value of American currency would no longer be measured in terms of a fixed amount of the precious metal. Instead, the dollar would find its worth in relation to other currencies according to the demand for it in world markets.

By taking America off the gold standard, Roosevelt was in effect encouraging a currency war. In May 1933, in the second of his famous "fireside chats" broadcast on radio to the American people, he continued to give support to the purposes of the conference and the

Presidential adviser Raymond Moley (left) with assistants returning by ship from the London Economic Conference, July 1933.

"stabilization of currencies." But within his administration there was division. The secretary of state, Cordell Hull (1871–1955), was a distinguished internationalist. He pleaded for international solutions, including a lowering of trade barriers in the form of protective tariffs, to the world's economic difficulties. But the assistant secretary of state, Raymond Moley (1886–1975), one of Roosevelt's longest-serving and most trusted advisers, was far less convinced of the internationalist approach.

Like Roosevelt, Moley believed in national solutions to national

Senator Hiram Johnson, who introduced a congressional act in 1934 barring debt-defaulting nations from borrowing in the U.S.

economic problems. Hull was the chairman of the American delegation to the London conference, but Moley was given the status of the president's special emissary. Open conflict between the two chief American representatives marred the conference. Cordell Hull—and indeed the conference itself—was sunk by Roosevelt's bombshell "Indianapolis statement" of July 3. From the deck of the cruiser *Indianapolis* the president announced his own opposition to the very idea of stabilized currencies and pressing upon Europeans the need for balanced budgets and domestic financial reforms.

The Drive for Exports

There was much to be said in defense of Roosevelt's position. By going off the gold standard, Great

Britain had lowered the value of the pound and gained an advantage in international trading markets. Roosevelt, too, wanted to boost American exports by lowering their cost to foreign buyers. By the middle of 1933 it was far from clear that the fall in the value of the dollar had been sharp enough to justify putting the American export trade at risk by an international currency agreement. At the forefront of Roosevelt's mind, too, was the damage that a currency-stabilization scheme might do to his New Deal efforts to raise prices, especially farm prices. Nevertheless, the president, at the head of the world's richest nation and the world's leading creditor, was severely censured by internationalists at home and abroad for failing to bring American leadership to the search for a world economic order. The Nazis and right-wing parties in the European democracies gleefully seized on the Indianapolis statement as support for the nationalist

sentiment that threatened once more to tear Europe apart.

In the background to the quarrel between the two schools of thought represented by Hull and Moley was a stark fact: By 1932 the value of American exports had dropped from their 1929 level of more than $5 billion to only about $1.6 billion. Hull's remedy was to encourage a freer international trade conducted in stable currencies. Moley and Roosevelt, on the other hand, the principal architects of the New Deal, preferred to find purely American remedies.

The Johnson Act

One example of the approach of Roosevelt and Moley was the Johnson Act of 1934, named after its chief creator, Senator Hiram Johnson of California (1866–1945). The act barred foreign governments that had failed to repay war debts to the United States from floating loans on the American financial markets.

Putting Down the Big Stick

FDR's Good Neighbor policy toward Latin America marked a significant departure from the overbearing attitude that had long characterized U.S. relations with its southern neighbors. Ironically, it was the president's cousin and White House predecessor, Theodore Roosevelt, who had most vividly personified American swagger, once memorably suggesting that the U.S. should "Speak softly and carry a big stick."

Rejecting the World Court

A measure of the strength of isolationist opinion in the United States was provided by the reaction to the establishment of the World Court in 1923. The court had only a voluntary jurisdiction. In other words, it could not hear cases unless they were submitted to it by an interested nation. Nor could citizens of one country be held to account before the court by an action brought by another country. But it was a creature of the League of Nations, a body so unpopular in the United States that the protocol of the court was ratified by the Senate in 1926 only with the addition of substantial qualifications.

After years of negotiations about those additions the Senate was again required to ratify the protocol in 1935. The newspaper publisher William Randolph Hearst (1863–1951) and the radio broadcaster Father Charles Coughlin (1891–1979), both of whom were leading isolationists familiar to every American, whipped up such antagonism against the court that protests against ratification rained on Capitol Hill. In just a few days senators received 200,000 telegrams opposing the

The opening session of the World Court at the Chicago Coliseum in 1925, while Congress was still debating U.S. ratification.

court. Staff had to carry them in wheelbarrows to the Senate Office building. The debate in the Senate was not distinguished for its intelligence or its attention to fact. "We are being rushed pell-mell," ranted Huey Long (1893–1935), "to get into this World Court so that Señor Ab Jap or some other something from Japan can pass upon our controversies." The White House, counting on victory, made little effort to counter the anticourt feeling, and the Senate, despite having a large Democratic majority, voted by only 52 to 36 in favor of ratification—seven votes short of the required two-thirds majority.

On the other hand, there were signs in 1934 that protectionist sentiment in Congress was weakening. The creation of the Export-Import Bank facilitated the extension of loans and financial credits to foreign buyers of American goods. At the same time, the Reciprocal Trade Agreements Act, which reduced protective tariffs, marked a step toward greater international free trade.

U.S. diplomacy in the mid-1930s was chiefly directed toward the pursuit of agreements that would reinforce the effect of New Deal legislation by stimulating economic activity within the United States. That was true even of the Good Neighbor policy as it was worked out in relation to Latin America, although in this case there were a number of factors all pointing in the same direction.

Colonel Fulgencio Batista, having overthrown the Cuban government in 1933, reads a message from the U.S. secretary of the Navy promising not to intervene.

THE GOOD NEIGHBOR POLICY

The times could hardly have been more favorable for ushering in a new era of cooperation between Latin America and the United States. For one thing, the danger of European meddling in the region—the original ground for the assertion of American responsibility for the whole of the Western Hemisphere in the Monroe Doctrine of 1823—was nonexistent while Europe was in economic crisis. The State Department was well aware of the high resentment felt by Latin Americans at U.S. intervention in their internal affairs over many years. At the same time, there was a growing sentiment in American circles, shared and encouraged by

the president, that heavy-handedness in Latin America did not sit easily with the United States' commitment to freedom and democracy. Political sense and political idealism came together in this case, and were supported by economic considerations since Roosevelt reasonably hoped that good relations would boost American trade with Latin America. The Reciprocal Trade Agreement Act of 1934, which authorized the president to make tariff reductions of up to 50 percent with countries willing to

reciprocate, had particular relevance for Latin American countries. Eighteen agreements were negotiated under the act over the next four years. They did little to correct the imbalance of trade from which the American economy was suffering, but to those poor Latin American countries that were heavily dependent on trade with the United States the act was decidedly welcome.

An End to Intervention

Tariff reductions went hand in hand with other economic measures that testified to Roosevelt's good neighborliness toward Latin America. Loans to assist the development of agriculture and industry were accompanied by a new reluctance to protect the interests of private American capital in Latin America by military threats or armed intervention. Shortly before taking office, Roosevelt was advised by Sumner Welles (1892–1961), who was to be placed in charge of Latin American affairs, that American policies should "never again result in armed intervention by the United States in a sister republic." Roosevelt

•

"…never again result in armed intervention by the United States in a sister republic."

•

heeded that advice. Thirty American ships were dispatched to the Cuban capital, Havana, after the overthrow of the government there in 1933, but an invasion was never contemplated.

Extreme Views over the Airwaves

No one in America was prepared for the national reaction to a startling radio broadcast that went out from Station WJR in Detroit on Sunday, October 30, 1930. Listeners tuned in, as they had been doing for four years, to hear the weekly religious talk from Father Charles Coughlin, the Canadian-born Roman Catholic priest from the parish of Royal Oak, Michigan. What they heard, in the rich, mellow tones and intimate manner that had won Coughlin a devoted following, was a diatribe against the international bankers who had brought the world to ruin and the communists who planned to take it over. Letters in their thousands, most of them adulatory, poured in on WJR. A new demagogue was born.

By the end of 1930 Coughlin was broadcasting on 17 CBS stations to an audience of 10 million. Never before had one man had so large an audience. By 1932, when he drummed the slogan "Roosevelt or ruin" into American ears, his weekly audience had grown to about 40 million, and his personal receipts—sent in by well-wishers—were reaching $20,000 a week.

Coughlin began as a rabid New Deal supporter, but by the end of 1934 he had broken with FDR and become one of his fiercest opponents. He also became a powerful voice for isolationism, with his own newspaper, *Social Justice*, and his own organization, the National Union for Social Justice. As the decade wore on, the NUSJ revealed itself to be a forum for the dissemination of extreme right-wing views: anti-League of Nations, antilabor, anticommunist, anti-Semitic. Increasingly attracted by the policies of Hitler and the Nazis, Coughlin devoted much of his energy after 1938 to keeping America out of the looming European war. But by then his flock was thinning. His last radio broadcast was aired in April 1940. Once powerful enough to be credited with a major role in getting Congress to reject the World Court, he lost influence with all but a hard core of anti-Semitic, isolationist followers who agreed with him that World War II was caused by a British-Jewish conspiracy with which Roosevelt was in cahoots. When the Japanese attack on Pearl Harbor gave isolationism an unpatriotic name, the radio priest slipped rapidly into obscurity.

The Cuban episode was the nearest that Roosevelt came to employing gunboat diplomacy in Latin America. His administration held back from intervening in quarrels over debt repayments to American commercial concerns. It also retreated from the American habit of intervening in the internal economic policies of Latin American states. In that regard the most eye-catching example was Roosevelt's refusal to come to the aid of the American-owned Standard Oil Company in Bolivia when its holdings were expropriated by the Bolivian government. When Mexico, too, nationalized American-owned oil companies within its borders,

Roosevelt contented himself with negotiating compensation for the owners. Business interests complained of the president's failure to support them, and even liberals, who for many years had argued for nonintervention in Latin America, protested that the hands-off policy adopted by the State Department allowed brutal dictators like Rafael Trujillo in the Dominican Republic to remain in power.

At the 1928 Pan-American conference in Havana Latin American governments had called for a formal diplomatic agreement enshrining the principle of nonintervention. The United States at the time had managed to forestall any such development. But by its

subsequent actions it demonstrated its acceptance of the principle. In 1934 the Platt Amendment of 1901, by the terms of which the United States had claimed the right to intervene in the affairs of Cuba since the end of the Spanish-American War, was canceled. The evacuation of Haiti in the same year meant that no American marines were posted anywhere on Latin American soil. In 1936 the United States also abandoned its right to intervene in the affairs of Panama. That same year at Buenos Aires the nations of the New World pledged themselves to consult together in the event of international war that posed a threat to the peace of the Western Hemisphere.

Senator Gerald Nye of North Dakota. The Nye Committee concluded that the U.S. had been duped into entering World War I.

Fortune published a sensational article on the armaments industry, with compromising details of the close links between European arms manufacturers and American politicians. Shortly after the article's publication the Senate established a committee to investigate the trade in arms. Gerald Nye, the Republican senator from North Dakota, was appointed chairman of the committee.

The Nye Committee

Nye was a prominent isolationist who had been loud in his demands for such a committee. In Stephen Rauschenberg he found a no-holds-barred investigator and chief counsel for the committee. Men of the stature of banker J. P. Morgan and the du Pont brothers were hauled before the committee. More from settled conviction than from the weight of testimony the Nye Committee concluded that President Woodrow Wilson had allowed wicked Wall Street bankers, in league with arms dealers, to drag America into World War I. It was the search for profits, not a concern to make the world safe for democracy, that had brought the United States in on the side of the Allies. "When Americans went into the fray," according to Nye, "they little thought that they were there and fighting to save the skins of America bankers who had bet too boldly on the outcome of the war and had two billions of dollars of loans to the Allies in jeopardy."

Democrats accused Nye of turning the investigation into a partisan Republican vendetta against a former Democratic

STAYING OUT OF EUROPEAN AFFAIRS

Greater cooperation with Latin America was one thing; involvement in the affairs of Europe was quite another. Despite the Italian seizure of Abyssinia (Ethiopia) in 1935 and Hitler's defiance of the Treaty of Versailles in reoccupying the Rhineland in 1936, and despite the impotence of the League of Nations in the face of those provocations, isolationist sentiment in the United States showed no signs of abating. Since the War of 1812 no foreign troops had ever invaded American soil, and the country's physical separation from Europe and Asia encouraged people to believe that they could escape the consequences of events in other parts of the world. It was widely believed that the United States could best serve the world as a beacon of peace and democracy. George Earle, the governor of Pennsylvania, advised Americans in 1935 to turn their eyes inward. "If the world is to become a wilderness of waste, hatred, and bitterness," he said, "let us all the more earnestly protect and preserve our own oasis of liberty."

The disillusionment bred in Americans by the slaughter and destruction of World War I and its ominous aftermath nourished a pacifist temper in the postwar generation (see Volume 1, Chapter 3, "The Return to Normalcy"). College students took part in anti-war demonstrations, and religious and pacifist organizations campaigned to have Reserve Officer Training Corps programs removed from campuses. In April 1935 students mounted a one-hour "strike for peace" at universities all over the country, three days after 50,000 veterans of World War I had taken part in a "march of peace" through Washington and laid wreaths at the graves of congressmen who had voted against the declaration of war in April 1917.

A powerful ingredient in the makeup of American isolationism was the belief that big business had played a major part in taking the United States into World War I, and that the same "merchants of death" who had sought to make profits from war were responsible for the dreadful legacy of the war, the Great Depression. In March 1934 the glossy financial magazine

president, but there is little doubt that the great publicity which the committee's proceedings attracted worked its effect on the public mind. The growing isolationist mood was reflected in the

•

"We are not going to get tangled up with their troubles in the days to come."

•

congressional majorities in favor of the Neutrality Act of 1935, designed to keep the U.S. out of any future European conflict.

In his address to Congress at the beginning of 1936 Roosevelt spoke darkly of the threats to peace that were growing in Europe. If war came, however, he insisted that America's only course was to follow the path of neutrality "and through example and all legitimate encouragement and assistance to persuade other nations to return to the ways of peace and goodwill." In Dallas that summer he offered those nations only "moral help." "We are not," he assured the American people, "going to get tangled up with their troubles in the days to come." The message was repeated at Lake Chautauqua in western New York in August. "We shun political commitments which might entangle us in foreign wars," Roosevelt said; "we avoid connection with the political activities of the League of Nations."

Most memorable of all was the deeply personal tone of a passage included in the Chautauqua speech. Roosevelt had never seen

active military service, but he had served as assistant secretary of the navy from 1913 to 1920: "I have seen war. I have seen war on land and sea. I have seen blood running from the wounded. I have seen men coughing out their gassed lungs. I have seen the dead in the mud. I have seen cities destroyed… I have seen children starving. I have seen the agony of mothers and wives. I hate war.

"I have passed unnumbered hours, I shall pass unnumbered hours, thinking and planning how war may be kept from this nation."

The following December Roosevelt gave a specially printed and autographed copy of the address to close friends as a Christmas present.

The Ethiopian Crisis

By that Christmas Roosevelt had already faced his first foreign crisis. In October 1935 Italian troops invaded Ethiopia. The invasion was entirely unprovoked. The Italian dictator, Benito Mussolini (1883–1945), was simply eager to acquire new territory. The League

of Nations looked to respond to his aggression by calling on all member states to place an embargo on the shipment of oil supplies to Italy. Such an embargo, intended to immobilize the Italian army and weaken the Italian economy, would be successful only if the United States, the world's largest oil-producer, agreed to take part in it. But Roosevelt's hands were tied.

Ethiopians prepare to defend their country against Italian invaders in 1935. The Western democracies responded weakly to the aggression.

The Ethiopian war had been looming for a year, and in the previous August Congress, fearful that the United States might be drawn into it, passed the first of five Neutrality Acts. The act required the president to place an embargo on the shipment of "arms, ammunitions, or implements of war" to nations at war and allowed him, at his discretion, to request Americans not to travel on ships belonging to the belligerent states. Roosevelt would have

Fierce fighting at Toledo in August 1936, where Spanish Nationalists were besieged by Republicans until relieved the following month.

preferred to have a discretionary power over the use of the embargo as well, but he approved of the main purpose of the bill; and since it was limited to only a six-month trial period, he did not hesitate to sign it.

As soon as Italy invaded Ethiopia, the president instructed his secretary of state, Cordell Hull, to issue a proclamation declaring American neutrality and putting the arms embargo into effect. Oil, however, was not included in the Neutrality Act, so Roosevelt was unable to lend American support to the League of Nations in its attempt to ban the sale of oil to Italy. Neither he nor Cordell Hull, however, was content to wash his hands of the affair. Together they strove to find an independent policy that would

Nationalist infantry celebrate the surrender of Madrid to their forces and thus victory in the Spanish Civil War, March 28, 1939.

somehow indicate the willingness of the United States to cooperate with the League.

Early in October Roosevelt instructed Hull to let the League know that, although the United States could not participate in an oil embargo, it would "go as far as laws allow to avoid giving material assistance to belligerents." At the end of the month Hull delivered a public statement in which he earnestly requested American

commercial interests not to engage in trade with the belligerents. On November 15, knowing that American trade with Italy had shown no signs of dropping off, he issued a list of goods—oil, copper, scrap iron, and steel among them—in which the American government would like trading to cease. "This class of trade," he announced, "is directly contrary to the policy of this government as announced in official statements of the president and secretary of state, as it is also contrary to the general spirit of the recent Neutrality Act."

Roosevelt's attempt to persuade American business not to trade with Italy became known as the "moral embargo." It failed in its purpose. In the last quarter of 1935 trade with Italy was up by 20 percent compared with the same period a year earlier. In the end the League itself failed to enforce an oil embargo on its members. Whether with full cooperation from the United States the League would have acted more decisively is guesswork, but the outcome was that the Western democracies

Japanese troops embark for the Chinese mainland, where by 1937 full-scale—although undeclared— war was under way.

stood by ineffectually wringing their hands while Italy absorbed Ethiopia. The forces of fascism had won an easy victory.

The Spanish Civil War

Hard on the heels of the Italian crisis civil war broke out in Spain (see box, page 38). The United States government, like those of all the Western democracies, kept clear of the war, which lasted from July 1936 until March 1939, when the Nationalists (fascists) under General Francisco Franco (1892–1975) finally emerged triumphant. From the beginning Franco's Nationalist forces were supplied with war materials, air power, and infantry by Germany and Italy. The Republican armies of the left received much less valuable assistance from the Soviet Union. Volunteers from the democracies went to Spain and fought on the Republican side in the International Brigades. But it was evident from the results of a

Gallup poll conducted early on in the conflict that the war aroused little interest in the United States. Two-thirds of the respondents said that they had no opinion on the war. At about the same time, Congress passed the third Neutrality Act of the 1930s, amending previous legislation in order to direct the law at the war in Spain. The arms embargo, which had previously applied only to international hostilities, was now extended to include internal rebellion and civil war. It was evidence of the continuing strength of isolationist sentiment in the U.S. that later in the 1937

session Congress voted to make the Neutrality Act a permanent part of American legislation.

JAPAN ON THE WARPATH

More worrying for Roosevelt than events in Spain was the escalating conflict between China and Japan. In 1931 the League of Nations had been powerless to prevent the Japanese conquest of Manchuria, the northernmost part of China. Since then Japan had gradually extended its occupation further and further into China, and by the middle of 1937 the two countries were engaged in full-scale hostilities. Neither side, however, had made a formal declaration of war against the other. Since the Neutrality Act allowed the president of the United States to invoke its provisions if he "found" a state of war to exist, Roosevelt was faced with a dilemma. To enforce the embargo would undoubtedly do harm to the Chinese forces, since they had fewer weapons and were far more dependent than the Japanese on foreign supplies. Roosevelt therefore decided to withhold a declaration of neutrality until China and Japan formally declared war against each other.

Another consideration influenced Roosevelt's Far East policy. The Neutrality Act included a

Polarized over Spain

While the Spanish Civil War may scarcely have registered in the minds of most Americans, for some it was the defining issue of the age. The insurgent General Franco was a fascist, but he was a staunch Roman Catholic too. So the Catholic hierarchy in the United States viewed the war as a struggle between Catholicism and communism. To liberal and left-wing intellectuals, many of them Jewish, and to union leaders Republican Spain represented constitutional democracy under attack from fascism, as seemed to be proved by the fact that Franco was supported by Hitler and Mussolini.

"cash-and-carry" clause that authorized the president to stop American businesses from selling to belligerents on credit terms. To invoke the clause in the Far East, however, would have been greatly to Japan's advantage, since Japan had financial resources far greater than China's. Roosevelt did not invoke the clause. Nor did he require, as the act allowed him to do, American ships to stop trading with nations at war. Again, to have done so would have benefited Japan, since Japan had more

American shipping might be subjected to Japanese attack; and when in August Roosevelt learned that a U.S. government vessel, the *Wichita*, had set out from Baltimore with a cargo of aircraft bound for China, he intervened. After forcing the *Wichita* to break its voyage at San Pedro, California, FDR announced a change of policy. Henceforth all government ships would be forbidden from carrying military supplies to China or Japan. Private ship owners were warned that to continue to

push to establish what it called a Greater East Asia Co-Prosperity Sphere—threatened America's military bases in the Philippines.

2. FDR BEGINS TO PREPARE THE NATION

That was the background to a major speech delivered by Roosevelt at Chicago on October 5, 1937. The president condemned the rising tide of "international lawlessness" in the world, especially acts of aggression committed without a declaration of war. It was, he repeated, his determination to pursue a policy of peace; but in a significant passage, he seemed to veer away from neutrality, away from the hope that America could remain a neutral beacon of liberty, aloof from events beyond its shores.

If international aggression continued to grow, he said, "let no

The USS Panay *sinking after being attacked by Japanese aircraft on December 12, 1937. The Japanese apologized for the incident.*

•

"let no one imagine that America will escape..."

•

merchant vessels than China and therefore more trading options. In effect, then, by officially ignoring the conflict, the president favored China. He was in tune with the public mood. Opinion polls showed that Americans condemned Japan's aggression and overwhelmingly supported China.

The president's Far East policy came under severe pressure in the summer of 1937, when Japan set up a blockade of Chinese ports. The blockade meant that

transport arms to the belligerents would be at their own risk.

The Chinese ambassador to Washington protested angrily, but FDR's decision did not reflect any loss of sympathy for China. What was uppermost in his mind was the need to avoid an international incident that might unavoidably draw the United States into the war in the Far East. He could not, of course, overlook the increasing pressure that Japanese aggression was placing on American freedom of action. Not only was the United States firmly in support of the integrity of China as an independent nation, but Japan's push to dominance in Southeast Asia—its

one imagine that America will escape, that it may expect mercy, that this Western Hemisphere will not be attacked, and that it will continue tranquilly and peacefully to carry on the ethics and the arts of civilization." On the contrary, "the moral consciousness of the world" must become "aroused to the cardinal necessity of honoring the sanctity of treaties, of respecting the rights and liberties of others, and of putting an end to acts of aggression."

The Chicago speech became known as the "Quarantine speech"

The Depth of Isolationist Sentiment

As Europe moved ever closer to war in 1938, an episode in Congress revealed that isolationist sentiment in the United States remained undimmed. Louis Ludlow, a congressman from Indiana, introduced an amendment to the U.S. Constitution to the effect that the United States could not go to war without the approval of the electorate as expressed in a national referendum. Roosevelt sent a message to Congress, read out by the speaker, in which he expressed his dismay at a proposal that would "cripple the president in his conduct of our foreign relations" and encourage foreign governments "to believe that they could violate American rights with impunity." Public opinion polls revealed that two-thirds of the American people backed the amendment, and support for it was powerful in the House of Representatives. A representative from Wisconsin argued that, since the Agricultural Adjustment Administration held plebiscites to ask farmers whether little pigs should be led to slaughter, it was all the more important that the people should be permitted a referendum vote to determine whether or not the sons and daughters of those same farmers should be led to slaughter on the battlefields of foreign countries.

The amendment received 209 votes in its favor and 188 against, but was lost because it failed to reach a two-thirds majority. Three-quarters of the Republican representatives and three-eighths of the Democrats voted in favor. The New Deal had raised alarms in the Republican Party of an overpowerful presidency, and some votes in the majority may have been influenced by the desire to curb the power of the White House. Even so, such strong support for so radical a proposal showed that the isolationist current, as late as 1938, was still running as swift as ever.

because the president compared international aggression to a spreading disease. Faced with an epidemic, communities joined together in a quarantine of the patients. The language was stronger than Roosevelt's practical commitment to collective security. When pressed to explain just what actions might be justified as constituting a "quarantine" of aggressor states, he talked about his government's determination to try to preserve peace.

Both at home and abroad observers were therefore bewildered in their attempt to grasp the true meaning of the speech. Historians, too, have been puzzled. Some of them have reached the conclusion that Roosevelt meant to signal a real change of policy, but that the extreme isolationist reaction that it produced in the

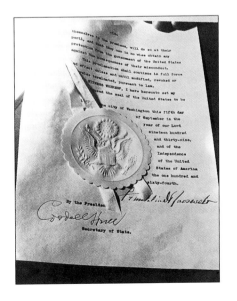

The last page of a formal proclamation of neutrality, signed by President Roosevelt and Secretary of State Cordell Hull on September 5, 1939. Germany's invasion of Poland on September 1 had plunged Europe into war.

United States compelled him to back down. Others have argued that Roosevelt was doing nothing more than sending up a trial balloon to see how far public opinion could be educated to the realities. Whatever FDR's motivation was, the Chicago speech was not followed by any change in American policy. American delegates to an international conference at Brussels, Belgium, in November 1937 made it clear that the United States would not contemplate the use of force, nor the application of economic sanctions, against Japan. The conference broke up, having achieved nothing.

Had America been in a less isolationist mood, an incident at the end of the year might have had dramatic consequences. On December 12, 1937, Japanese aircraft sank the USS *Panay*, a small

German troops occupy Vienna on March 12, 1938. The following day Adolf Hitler proclaimed the union of Austria and Germany.

gunboat belonging to the American Yangtze River patrol. Americans sighed with relief when the Japanese government apologized and offered to pay compensation to the victims. Japan had throughout 1937 been "accidentally" bombing American churches, missions, hospitals, and schools in China. The Japanese objective was to rid China of an American presence. Americans, according to a Gallup poll of January 1938, were happy to get out. More than two-thirds of the respondents favored a complete American withdrawal—Asiatic fleet, marines, missionaries, and every other American organization—from China.

The inability of the international powers to bring peace to the Far East exposed the inadequacy of those instruments of collective security, above all the League of Nations, which had come into being in the decade after World War I.

HITLER MOVES TOWARD WAR

In Europe the hopes for peace were also diminishing. Hitler had ridden roughshod over the Treaty of Versailles in occupying the Rhineland and in rearming Germany. Those were matters in which the United States, not having been a signatory to the treaty, had little say. But Hitler's aggression in 1938 could not go unnoticed by American policy-makers. In March German troops invaded Austria, and (admittedly to the delight of a majority of Austrians) Hitler incorporated his native country into the German Reich. That bold move went unchallenged by the democracies. In September they faced a graver crisis, provoked by Hitler's demand that the Sudetenland province of Czechoslovakia, the majority of whose inhabitants were German-speaking, become part of Germany.

Those people who hoped to stave off war by appeasing Hitler had their last triumph at the Munich meeting at the end of September (see box, page 40). France and Great Britain capitulated to Hitler, and Czechoslovakia was violated. What was Roosevelt's role in that final, fateful victory for appeasement? There was a suggestion from William Bullitt, the American ambassador to Paris, that the president might put himself forward as a neutral arbitrator to settle the dispute. Roosevelt did not take the suggestion seriously. On September 27 he appealed to Hitler to take part in an international conference to settle the dispute. Then, a day later, when he learned that the meeting in Munich was to take place, he sent a telegram to the British prime minister, Neville Chamberlain. "Good man" was all it said—and those words of encouragement have been interpreted both as support for defiance of Hitler and support for appeasement. Whatever Roosevelt meant was largely academic to events: His words almost certainly had no effect on proceedings.

The Munich Agreement

When the Munich meeting had done its work, and Czechoslovakia was sacrificed to avoid immediate war, there is no doubt that most American people, like most of the British, breathed a sigh of relief. Sumner Welles declared that the way had been opened to "a new world order based upon justice and upon law." President Roosevelt himself told a senior official at the State Department that he was "not a bit upset over the final result."

The Munich agreement nevertheless seems to have initiated a change of direction in Roosevelt's approach to the outside world. In his Quarantine speech he had hinted at the possibility of a war from which the United States would not be able to hide. In October 1938 he began to make preparations for such a war. He met with senior military advisers at the White House, and together they drew up plans to develop the aircraft industry so that it could provide British and French forces with the help that they needed and also give the United States a 10,000-strong air force. In November the president asked Congress for $300 million to finance the program. At the same time, he gave his approval to the formation of the Atlantic Squadron of the U.S. Navy. Finally, he decided to bolster what he called "the North-South American axis." In December an American delegation attended the Conference of American States in Lima and agreed, along with the

governments of Latin America, that neither they nor the United States should go to war in the Western Hemisphere without consulting one another. That agreement became known as the Lima Declaration.

As the fateful year of 1939 opened—the year that would bring war in Europe—it was evident that Roosevelt was preparing himself for the day when he might have to do battle against the largely isolationist temper of his countrymen. In his address to Congress on January 4 he spoke of coming trials: "There comes a time in the affairs of men when they must prepare to defend, not in their homes alone, but in the tenets of faith and humanity on which their churches, their governments, and their very civilization are founded. The defense of religion, of democracy, and of good faith among nations is the same fight. To save one we must make up our minds to save all."

A West Coast hangar where P-38 Lightning fighter aircraft are being manufactured during World War II. After Pearl Harbor the U.S. was totally committed to Allied victory.

4

THE ROAD TO WAR

When war broke out in Europe in September 1939, both the government and the people of the United States were determined not to get involved in another bloodbath like World War I. Over the next two years, however, the pressure of events prevented the U.S. from standing idly on the sidelines, and President Roosevelt edged the nation closer and closer to the Allied cause.

In September 1939, when World War II began in Europe, the United States remained neutral. Neutrality laws passed over the previous four years made it illegal for U.S. corporations or the government to sell weapons to any of the countries that were at

President Roosevelt appealing to Congress to modify the neutrality laws, September 26, 1939, three weeks after war began in Europe.

war. It was illegal for the government to loan money to any of the warring countries to help them pay for their war efforts. It was illegal for any American ships, civilian or military, to enter a war zone. It was also illegal for American citizens to travel there in foreign ships (see Chapter 3, "Foreign Policy").

Although the United States remained officially at peace for another two years, the situation changed radically in the inter-

vening period. By the time the Japanese attack on the Pacific Fleet base at Pearl Harbor in December 1941 brought America into the war, the U.S. was sending massive supplies to Germany's enemies, American sailors had been killed in action, and the United States had become committed to policies that worked against both Germany and Japan. Even though the U.S. had therefore moved a long way from neutrality in both the Atlantic and Pacific theaters by December 1941, in the end it was not an American choice to go to war against Japan or Germany. Japan attacked Pearl Harbor, and Germany declared war on the United States in support of its Japanese ally. America's declarations of war were in response to those acts.

1. THE POLICY OF ISOLATIONISM

In 1939 most Americans supported "isolationism." This was the view that the United States should concentrate its resources completely on its own needs, and that it could survive quite happily and prosperously by doing so. The United States had helped Britain and France in World War I and, isolationists asked, what had that achieved?

Not Neutral in Sympathies

Almost all Americans blamed Nazi Germany for starting World War II and wanted Britain and France to win it. But at the same time, opinion polls also showed that most Americans thought their country had been mistaken to fight in World War I, and more than 90 percent wanted to stay out of this new war, too. The neutrality laws of the mid-1930s were designed to match these wishes and ensure that America did not get dragged in by accident.

Tens of thousands of young Americans had died in that war, and afterward the Europeans had shown their gratitude for that help by defaulting on their debts to the U.S. If the Europeans were homicidal (or suicidal) enough to

go to war again, that was their problem, and Americans were better off out of it.

Most isolationists did not deny the unpleasant nature of the German or Japanese regimes in the years before 1939, though some thought that the Germans were a lot better than the Soviet communists. Most Americans were shocked by the Nazis' persecution of Germany's Jews and by the brutality and illegality of Germany's attacks on peaceful neighboring countries. Japan's attacks on China were seen as equally vile and unprovoked. Tens of thousands of Chinese had died in the December 1937 "rape of Nanking," for example, which was widely reported in the U.S. But none of that made these problems America's affair. Americans had troubles enough of their own; and if the Europeans or Asians were determined to fight, how could the U.S. be expected to stop them?

OPPOSING VIEWS

The leading isolationist group in 1940 and 1941 was the Committee to Defend America

Nazi SA picket a Jewish warehouse in Berlin in April 1933, giving immediate notice of the new regime's virulent anti-Semitism.

First. This organization was supported by a wide range of people. It was largely financed by Henry Ford and other ultrarich businessmen, but its supporters included Republicans and Democrats, and conservatives and liberals of all classes and backgrounds. The small American Communist Party also backed the organization from August 1939 to June 1941, when the Nazis and the Soviets were allies. Prominent politicians like Senator William Borah of Idaho were among its leaders, and the famed aviator Charles Lindbergh was one of its top public speakers (see Volume 1, Chapter 4, "The Roaring Twenties"). America First's main slogan was "Fortress America," the belief that the United States was strong enough to stand alone whatever Hitler did in Europe.

President Roosevelt and his administration saw things differently. He believed that

Events of the European War, 1939–1941

War in Europe began on September 1, 1939, with a German attack on Poland. Great Britain and France declared war on Germany two days later because they now realized that the German dictator, Adolf Hitler, was a deadly menace, and that it was not possible to make any sort of deal with him that he would keep. Canada and the other members of the British Commonwealth also declared war on Germany. Even so, Poland was quickly defeated, and in the spring of 1940 Germany attacked west and north, first rapidly conquering Denmark and Norway, and then the Netherlands, Belgium, and France. France surrendered in June, but Great Britain fought on. Italy joined the war on Germany's side just before France surrendered.

In the fall of 1940 the British Royal Air Force forced the Germans to postpone their planned invasion of England. Britain would never be invaded, but Germany's submarine (U-boat) force began making more and more damaging attacks on the cargo ships that Britain relied on to bring food and other supplies essential for survival and for continuing the war.

In the early months of 1941 German victories continued. German forces overran Yugoslavia and Greece and reinforced the Italian army in Libya (an Italian colony then), gaining the upper hand in battles with British forces based in Egypt. Hitler's main plan for 1941, however, was for an all-out attack on the Soviet Union.

Hitler had made a temporary alliance with the Soviet dictator, Josef Stalin, just before attacking Poland in 1939, but now he broke his word to Stalin—as he had to everyone else. German tanks crashed across the Soviet border on June 22, 1941. By early December they had reached the outskirts of the Soviet capital, Moscow, but were counterattacked and defeated there by the Red Army. This would be as close as Germany would come to winning the war.

The German army marches through Saarbrücken, on the German-French border in summer 1940, having overwhelmed France.

American interests would be badly damaged if the Germans or Japanese succeeded in their aims. The U.S. benefited greatly by trade and cultural contacts with Europe and from investments and other commercial connections with China and Asia. If Germany came to dominate Europe, that might even pose a threat of a direct attack on the United States, and U.S. territories in the Pacific were already being menaced by the Japanese. Roosevelt said that if America tried to survive as "a lone island in a world dominated by the philosophy of force," then the American people would effectively be in prison, "fed through the bars from day to day by the contemptuous, unpitying masters of other continents."

In addition, the opponents of isolationism said, one of the reasons why the situation in Europe and Asia had gotten so bad was because the U.S. had not used its power and influence to help prevent this. It was the worst of both worlds, they believed, to speak out against German and Japanese aggression and still to do nothing about it. That could only anger America's likely enemies and hurt friends—as Neville Chamberlain, Britain's prime minister in the critical years leading up to war, bitterly commented, "It is always best and safest to count on nothing from the Americans but words."

Roosevelt, however, did not think that the answer was to go to war, even if he could have persuaded the American people in 1939 that that was the right thing to do. Roosevelt had said sincerely in prewar speeches that he hated war, but he also recognized the evils of Nazism and Japanese militarism, and thought it would be morally wrong, as well as against America's interests, to do nothing to prevent Japanese or German successes. When war began in Europe, Roosevelt therefore decided to do as much as he could to help Germany's enemies, working to change American law and public opinion as necessary to achieve this. The U.S. would aim to do enough to help the Europeans defeat Germany but without actually going to war. The U.S. would also try to avoid war with Japan. Instead, Japan would be met with negotiations that would gain

•

*"It is always best...
to count on nothing
from the Americans
but words."*

•

enough time for U.S. military strength to be built up to a level that Japan would not dare to attack. In this way neither Germany nor Japan would achieve its aggressive objectives, but the U.S. would, Roosevelt hoped, also avoid having to fight. The details of these policies changed greatly between September 1939 and December 1941, but in general terms their aims held good throughout.

Roosevelt knew that strong U.S. policies might provoke a German or Japanese attack, but he also thought that the real issue was whether Germany or Japan wanted war with the United States. If they did, there would be little he could do about it. As recent history had shown, both were quite capable of starting a war whenever they wanted one (see Chapter 2, "The Victory of Authoritarianism"). In that case the task for the American government would be to try to ensure that war began at a time and in circumstances that were as favorable as possible.

THE PRESIDENT'S PROMISE

In his campaign to win a third term in 1940 Roosevelt promised repeatedly that he would not send U.S. soldiers to fight in foreign wars unless America was attacked first—and that was a promise that he kept. Roosevelt left out the "unless" part in one speech and was never allowed to forget it by his political enemies, but their charges of broken promises on that count diverted attention from more important points that historians today now debate. How far did Roosevelt's policies and actions, some of them kept secret from the American people, give the Japanese and Germans little alternative but to attack, and was this what Roosevelt secretly intended? Or were Germany and Japan so determined to get what they wanted that the only real choice for America was either to fight or to give in completely?

CASH AND CARRY

President Roosevelt had opposed (but not vetoed) the neutrality laws when they were introduced because he thought that tying the

U.S. Military Power in 1939

In 1939 the U.S. was not a military superpower. The U.S. Army was many times smaller than its German, French, or Soviet equivalents, and poorly equipped. Reference books listed it as 13th in size in the world—ahead of Portugal but behind Bulgaria. The air force was not an independent service but a modestly sized corps within the Army and had fewer than 200 modern combat planes, as compared to Germany's 4,000. Fortunately, the U.S. Navy at least was powerful in world terms. It was very slightly smaller than Britain's Royal Navy, the world's largest, and about 40 percent bigger than the Japanese navy. However, the U.S. Navy was not powerful enough to fight the Japanese in the Pacific with any hope of success if it also had to keep substantial forces in the Atlantic. This might be necessary to support the British or, as looked possible for a time in 1940, if Germany defeated Britain and France and got control of their ships, to oppose a massive German-led force.

The Battle of Britain

In order to invade Britain, the Germans needed to transport a large army across the English Channel, and this required aerial superiority to counter the threat of the powerful British navy. In August 1940 the German Luftwaffe and the Royal Air Force began fighting a battle over the skies of southern England. Despite being outnumbered, the RAF fought off the invaders, and by September it was apparent that the Germans could not gain their objective. The invasion was called off.

British fighter pilots sprint to their waiting planes during the Battle of Britain, August–September 1940. Their heroism saved Britain.

government's hands in this way made it more difficult for him to act in America's best interests. When the European war began in 1939, he therefore immediately set about getting the neutrality laws changed. Roosevelt doubted if Britain and France were strong enough to stand up to Germany on their own because their armament programs had a long way to go to catch up on the lead that the Nazis had seized earlier in the decade. He decided that they must be permitted to buy arms in the U.S.

Roosevelt's proposals were bitterly opposed by his political enemies, but an amended law, usually called "cash and carry," was passed by Congress and signed into law on November 4, 1939. It allowed any country at war to buy weapons from U.S. corporations, provided they paid for them in cash (not by loans raised in the United States) and then transported them from the United States in the purchasing country's own ships. This supposedly applied equally to all the belligerents, but it was obviously designed to help Britain and France since the simple facts of geography and Britain's powerful navy would effectively prevent any such supplies reaching the Germans.

The Allies Rush to Buy

The British and French set up purchasing missions in the U.S. within days of the cash-and-carry law coming into effect and soon began issuing orders for aircraft, guns, and much more. It would, however, take some time before the orders were turned into substantial deliveries since American industries were not yet equipped for large-scale arms production. One benefit of the process that Roosevelt and his advisers recognized was that as American industries equipped themselves to fulfill the foreign orders, they would also be getting ready to build more weapons for America's own armed forces. Such rearmament they considered vital at a clearly dangerous time. Congress did not necessarily agree—in April 1940 the House cut the armed forces budget and canceled orders for two-thirds of the aircraft originally planned.

During that same month, April 1940, Germany attacked Denmark and Norway, two more countries that Americans could plainly see had done nothing to deserve such violent treatment. Since Greenland and Iceland had ties to Denmark, the fall of Denmark brought the threat of a German presence much closer to North America than before, creating another reason for Americans to worry. Then in June France was completely overwhelmed by a German invasion. The British army was evacuated home from the French port of Dunkirk but had to leave

virtually all its tanks and guns behind. Germany seemed set to win the war very soon and dominate the whole of central and western Europe.

TWO-OCEAN NAVY

This prospect changed many minds in the United States. Congress now agreed to huge increases in the military budget. Previously American defense planners had assumed that they would only have to fight one major enemy at any time, and the most likely candidate in recent years had been Japan. Now the Navy in particular would need to have sufficient forces to be able to fight in both the Atlantic and the Pacific. In July 1940 the Two Ocean Navy Bill passed into law, authorizing new ships that would almost double the Navy's size, a stunning increase for any nation to plan in peacetime.

The fear that Britain might be on the point of defeat gradually receded in the late summer and fall of 1940, as the Royal Air Force successfully beat off the German Luftwaffe and won the Battle of Britain. By then, though, the British government had told Roosevelt's administration of another problem: They were running out of cash and could not go on paying for the arms and other supplies they needed for more than a few months longer. After that, unless they could borrow or make other arrangements, they probably could not even go on fighting at all, never mind win the war.

THE ELECTION OF 1940

Roosevelt at this point was running for an unprecedented third presidential term. He was doing so as much to protect the New Deal against its Republican

and Democratic enemies as to continue the active foreign policies he had developed. Although his objectives were therefore as much connected with the domestic front as with the critical foreign situation, in the 1940 election campaign Roosevelt tried hard to portray himself as the national leader too deeply concerned with defending his country to bother with party politics. As part of this strategy Roosevelt brought prominent Republicans into his cabinet, Frank Knox (1874–1944) as secretary of the Navy and Henry Stimson (1867–1950) as secretary of war.

Roosevelt's opponent in the election was not one of the Republican isolationists, however, but the very popular political novice Wendell Willkie (1892–1944), who also supported giving increasing aid to the British. But it did not make Willkie's campaign any easier that on the one hand he criticized Roosevelt for neglecting the nation's defenses and on the other accused him of being too ready to

Rival supporters during the presidential election campaign of 1940. Crucially, Willkie supported FDR's policy of aiding Britain.

force the nation to go to war. To make matters more difficult yet for the Republicans, unemployment declined as Britain's arms purchases and America's own rearmament created more and more jobs. Roosevelt would win a comfortable victory in November, with 54.8 percent of the vote against Willkie's 44.8 percent.

COMING TO BRITAIN'S AID

While the election campaign was at its height, Willkie supported the next important move that Roosevelt decided to make. This was the so-called Destroyers-for-Bases agreement made in early September, whereby the U.S. transferred 50 old U.S. Navy destroyers to the British (for use in fighting the German U-boats) in return for the U.S. being given leases on various bases in British territories in the Western

U.S. Navy flying cadets on the training course. By 1940 the United States was rapidly building up its armed forces in the event of war.

(1874–1965). The administration did not simply take the British word for this. It checked and made sure that the last British assets in the United States were sold off cheap to U.S. corporations before it would go any further. On December 17 Roosevelt held a press conference in which he introduced the next stage in his policy, which soon became known as Lend-Lease.

Roosevelt compared the war in Europe to a fire in a neighbor's house. It would make sense even from a selfish standpoint to help your neighbor put the fire out, since the fire could spread to your house if you did not. In those circumstances, if you had a hose, you would lend it to your neighbor at once and worry about the cost of the hose later. What this meant in terms of the situation was that Roosevelt wanted the U.S. government to pay for the things the British needed and lend them to the British for now. Then, at the

Hemisphere. There was also a promise from the British that if Britain was successfully invaded by the Germans, they would sail the powerful Royal Navy to Canada and not surrender it to German control. Roosevelt made this deal by executive authority without allowing Congress to vote on it, which outraged his isolationist opponents. It was, however, an important step in accustoming the American people to working with the British against what increasingly looked like a common enemy.

There was no question that the next important step had to be passed by Congress. It was the introduction of the draft for the first time in the nation's peacetime history. Bitterly opposed by the isolationists, the Selective Service Act, which set this system up, was passed by Congress in mid-September, and the first drafts were balloted at the end of

October. This was the basis for a huge expansion in the strength of the Army.

LEND-LEASE

Shortly after the 1940 elections British representatives in the U.S. went public with the information that their country was virtually bankrupt, and this was backed up by detailed explanations to Roosevelt from British Prime Minister Winston Churchill

A "Buy British" display on New York's Fifth Avenue. Americans' sympathies were aroused by Britain's resolute self-defense.

Vast quantities of truck, tractor, aircraft, and other machine parts on a New Jersey pier, awaiting shipment to Britain in early 1940.

end of the war the British could either return them or pay for any they wanted to keep. Roosevelt explained in one of his fireside chat radio broadcasts that he wanted the U.S. in this way to become the "arsenal of democracy."

The passage of the Lend-Lease bill was fiercely opposed by the isolationists in Congress. Senator Burton Wheeler (1882–1975) of Montana, for example, warned that it would mean "every fourth American boy being plowed under," but the bill was eventually passed by 250–165 in the House and 60–31 in the Senate. The president signed it on March 11, 1941, and Congress passed the law granting the first $7 billion to finance it by the end of the month. Though Congress retained control of the financing of Lend-Lease, the president was given discretion to choose what the money was spent on and who, the British or anyone else, would get the supplies.

Though it would take some time for Lend-Lease supplies to start to flow to Britain, the act and the huge sums of money involved were a clear public statement of America's willingness to support the British. In secret there were also other steps toward cooperation. The most important of them were probably the series of

•

"…every fourth American boy being plowed under"

•

discussions known as ABC1, for American-British Conversations 1, between top British and U.S. commanders. They recommended to their respective governments that if the two countries had to go to war against Germany and Japan, the defeat of Germany should be the top-priority objective. The two countries also shared other secret information. The U.S. gave the

British access to decodes of Japan's diplomatic messages, and the British gave the U.S. the information they were getting from Germany's codes (see box, page 76), as well as technical details in radar and other fields in which British scientists had the lead.

The most dramatic developments in U.S. foreign policy in the period from September 1939 until the spring of 1941 were therefore based around and caused by the events of the European war. But that was not to say that the situation in Asia and the Pacific had not changed, nor that events there were not related to events in Europe. Japan was set on a policy of expansion but had a choice of targets and possible enemies, and choosing where to strike might be governed in part by what was happening in Europe.

2. JAPANESE MILITARISM
The way that Japan was governed seemed superficially to be similar to the situation in other monarchies like Great Britain, but in fact there were substantial and important differences. In Britain governments could only be appointed after winning proper democratic elections, and they had complete and unchallenged control of the country's foreign policy and of the military.

This was not the situation in Japan (see Chapter 1, "Economics and Political Extremism"). In Japan the army and the navy ministers in the government had to be generals and admirals on the active service list. If the top men in either service did not like government policy, they simply had their representative resign and refused to provide another one until the government was changed. Both the army and navy

Japanese cadets at training school. By the late 1930s Japan was increasingly committed to gaining its objectives by military force.

also had the right to suggest policies to the emperor separately from the government. The emperor's constitutional role was entirely formal, and his consent to such proposals was given automatically; but once his consent was given, the proposals in effect became imperial commands that had to be obeyed. The army and navy were therefore laws unto themselves. They did not even have to tell the government (or each other) what their plans and dispositions were.

Japan's military was trained to be tough and unyielding, never surrendering, never retreating, never considering the human cost of whatever it might do. From the 1920s, in addition to its political powers, the military took more and more control over Japan's educational system, so that these aggressive military values came to have far more influence in Japanese society as a whole than they had ever done before. From

the early 1930s maps in school textbooks showed the British, French, and Dutch colonies in Asia as being rightfully part of Japan's empire, for example.

THE VIEW FROM JAPAN

Japanese generally were in no doubt what their country's problems were. Japan had few of the natural resources and raw materials essential to support a modern industrial and military economy; it did not even grow enough food for its own population. Japan had no oil of its own, no rubber, little tin or nickel or any number of other important minerals. Some of what Japan needed came directly from America, including the majority of its machine tools and most of the scrap metal that went to make new steel for weapons. Most of the rest came from the European colonies of Southeast Asia: rubber from Malaysia, oil from the Dutch East Indies, and much more.

Japan's leaders also had no doubt that despite these problems, their country's destiny was to rule in Asia. They thought that, partly on racist grounds, they had been unfairly denied their just rewards for success in previous wars and for their support of the Allies in World War I. They saw nothing wrong with taking what they wanted by force.

Japan aimed for what economists call autarky for its empire, that is to say, complete self-sufficiency without needing to rely on trading with or importing anything from the rest of the world—similar in a way to what the isolationists wanted for the United States. Japan's leaders, however, did not agree on the steps necessary to achieve this. The army had dragged the country into war

Asia and the Pacific in 1939

The map of Asia and the Pacific region was very different in 1939 from what it would become only 10 years later. Britain, France, and the Netherlands all had extensive colonies in the area. Britain ruled Malaya, Burma, India (including modern India, Pakistan, and Bangladesh), Sri Lanka (Ceylon, as it was then), and parts of Borneo. France ruled Indochina (modern Vietnam, Cambodia, and Laos), and present-day Indonesia was the Dutch East Indies. The United States, too, controlled various territories. As a U.S. commonwealth the Philippines had its own government and was due to become fully independent in 1946, but it was still in effect an American colony. In Southeast Asia only Thailand, then usually called Siam, was independent, though it was at the time under strong Japanese influence.

China and Japan were the most powerful Asian countries. They had been fighting each other, with varying degrees of intensity, since Japan's conquest of Manchuria in 1931. Japan had won most of the battles but had not been able to defeat the Chinese completely. By the time the European war began, Japan's empire in China included many of the richest and most productive parts of the country. Japan had also fought numerous battles with the Soviets along the borders between the Soviet Union and Japanese-controlled areas of China throughout the 1930s. They never led to full-scale war but they convinced the Japanese to look south rather than north for expansion.

As well as large and efficient armies in China and at home Japan also had the world's third-largest navy (after Britain and the U.S.). Japan's industries were well developed and its economy potentially very strong.

Control of China was contested between the Nationalists, or Kuomintang, led by

Chiang Kai-shek, and the Communists led by Mao Zedong (Mao Tse-tung). The Nationalists were recognized by the U.S. and other countries as the legitimate government, but their leadership was riddled with corruption, and their army was badly equipped, motivated, and trained. It seemed to many observers that Chiang's strategy was to do as little as possible against the Japanese while deploying his strongest units to make sure the Communists did not increase their territory. The Communists seemed to want to fight the Japanese energetically, partly because they thought this would gain them support from other Chinese in their quarrel with the Nationalists.

U.S. poster saluting the fighting qualities of the Filipinos after the Japanese overran the Philippines in December 1941.

that month the United States gave the required notice that it would not be renewing the U.S.–Japanese trade agreement (dating back to 1911) when it expired during 1940. Since some 40 percent of Japanese exports and 60 percent of imports were to or from America, this was a serious threat.

NORTH OR SOUTH?

The military could not admit they had gotten Japan into a mess; but the longer they kept fighting in China, the more imported steel and oil they needed, and the worse the mess got. Retreating or making peace was unthinkable, so the only way out was to grab yet more territory and resources in the hope that that would some-how solve the problem. But where should Japan attack next?

Japan had a long history of clashes with the Soviet Union in northeast China along the borders between Japanese-held territory there and the Far Eastern parts of the USSR. There had been numerous skirmishes and a num-ber of major battles in this region through the 1930s, and many Japanese army officers saw the

first in Manchuria (see box, page 22) and then in many parts of China. At first this war had seemed economically beneficial, since military spending had helped the Japanese economy recover from the effects of the Depression, but in the longer term this was an illusion. The war in China dragged on, and Japan was no nearer winning it. And the war also in-creased Japan's need for imported oil, steel, and other raw materials to supply its fighting forces and arms industries.

In July 1939 these problems began to seem much worse, for in

Japanese soldiers cross a makeshift bridge in the course of conquering Nanking, December 1937.

The famous Burma Road, one of China's supply lifelines. In the summer of 1940 Japanese pressure forced the British to close the road.

Co-Prosperity Sphere

The Japanese sometimes tried to give their aims a gentler appearance. Prime Minister Prince Konoe Fumimaro spoke in 1938 of a New Order in East Asia, and in 1940 and later he and other Japanese leaders proposed a Greater East Asia Co-Prosperity Sphere. This was a vague Japanese-led commonwealth from which all Asians would benefit— once the European colonial powers were out of the way. "Asia for the Asiatics" became the slogan, but the brutal military tyranny that the Japanese imposed in all the territories that they occupied showed where the truth behind the fine words lay. Japan planned to conquer and then exploit an empire and did not care what means were used to do so.

were badly beaten. And in August, just as the Japanese were being forced to retreat, the Soviets made their deal with the Nazis in Europe, making it easier for them to send yet more of their troops to the Far East should they need to. The little-known battles of No-monhan therefore turned out to be a decisive turning point in history, for the Japanese army and government now looked more seriously for alternatives to a strike to the north. They would turn south for new conquests in China, the East Indies, and the Pacific; war against the Soviet Union, they decided, was not in their interests.

JAPAN CHANGES COURSE

Japan's aggression in China during the 1930s had brought about a gradual and growing response from the United States and other countries. Financial assistance and supplies were given to the Chinese and delivered via French Indo-china and (British) Burma. They did not amount to very much, but the Japanese believed that they were instrumental in persuading the Chinese to keep fighting. And since extension or at the very least

consolidation of their hold over China was the nonnegotiable bottom line in Japan's foreign policy, they were something the Japanese could not tolerate.

Both the United States and Japan were cautious from the start of the European war until the German victories in the spring of 1940. The Japanese saw them as an opportunity, and Prince Konoe (1891–1945) returned as prime minister in a more militant government. Britain, France, and the Netherlands were either weakened or left powerless. But it was not an opportunity that would last forever, since Japan could not possibly hope to match the expansion in U.S. strength that the Two-Ocean Navy Act (1940) would bring in a year or two—even though it was aimed at the German rather than the Japanese threat.

In mid-July 1940, under Japanese pressure at the worst moment for their country in the war, the British agreed to close the Burma Road. They would reopen it three months later in slightly better times, but the closure was a sign that if anyone was going to stand up to Japan, it would have to

Soviets as their natural enemy. Japan, they believed, should strike north against the communist giant.

Then, in the late spring and summer of 1939 there was a particularly fierce series of battles in the Nomonhan area, on the border between Soviet-backed Mongolia and Japanese-occupied China. It is not clear who started the fighting, but after both sides sent reinforcements, the Japanese

American P-40s delivered to the Chinese to help them in their war with Japan. The Japanese were determined to cut off such supplies.

The signing of the Tripartite Pact between Germany, Italy, and Japan, September 1940. It said an attack on one would be an attack on all.

supply route through Indochina and securing the raw materials they wanted by war in Malaysia and the East Indies. And if that meant war with the United States, then so be it. This was not yet an irrevocable decision to attack Pearl Harbor—the Japanese still had plenty of opportunities to step back from the brink —but it was the moment when, at Japan's choice, war between the United States and Japan became far more likely than not.

ADVANCE INTO INDOCHINA

In mid-September 1940 the Japanese took the first step in this new plan when they moved troops into northern Indochina after negotiating an agreement with the

be the United States. A week later the United States imposed a partial embargo on exports to Japan on items including some fuels and oil-related products.

At the end of July 1940 the Japanese government formally adopted the twin policy for "ending the China Incident," as they called it, of blocking the

---

Did FDR Have a Master Plan?

From 1939 to December 1941 Roosevelt claimed that he was reacting to Axis and Japanese aggression. However, some historians believe that he had a blueprint for the future of the world, and that his actions demonstrate a clear working toward it. Their argument starts with the weakness of the European democracies in the late 1930s. France and Britain were too worried by the threat of communist world revolution to form an alliance with the Soviet Union to contain Hitler, and so could not prevent Hitler expanding Germany's frontiers and dominating Europe by force.

Given that Hitler's success was mirrored by the aggression of Japan in Asia, the argument continues, Roosevelt could see that it was necessary for the United States to intervene to prevent fascist or authoritarian domination of the whole Eurasian landmass. Therefore he steadily maneuvered the

United States into a position where it was likely to be the victim of an act of war by Germany or, more likely, Japan. Roosevelt's position was made somewhat easier by the fact that Hitler had attacked Stalin's Soviet Union in June 1941, which meant that the world's biggest army was arrayed against Nazism. If the Soviet Union could hold out against the first year of German attacks, then substantial U.S. aid would begin to tell in Stalin's favor.

Proponents of this argument then frequently go on to claim that Roosevelt's view of the world he was creating involved ending the colonial empires of Holland, France and Britain to establish a more widely democratic world in which the principles of Roosevelt's United States would reign supreme, but that in so doing he was prepared to allow Stalin almost a free hand over much of Europe and mainland Asia.

French authorities. The new French government established after the German victory in June had no power to resist this, and in any case it was eager to make the best deal it could with Germany and Germany's friends. In reply to the Japanese move the United States imposed an embargo on exports of scrap iron and steel to Japan. The tit-for-tat sequence of escalating responses that would lead to war had begun in earnest. The United States extended its embargo to cover more categories of goods in December, and in the meantime the Japanese also failed to buy all they oil they had hoped for in negotiations with the Dutch East Indies authorities, though they still continued to receive large amounts for the moment.

ALLIANCE WITH GERMANY

Part of Japan's policy was to develop the rather vague alliance they had had with Germany since the anticommunist Anti-Comintern Pact of 1936. On September 27, 1940, Germany, Italy, and Japan signed a treaty known as the Tripartite Pact in which they promised to declare war on any country that attacked any of the three. This agreement was obviously directed against any threat from the United States. The Japanese saw it as preventing the United States standing up to them by threatening that any U.S. action would mean fighting a European war as well. For their part, the Germans were delighted to encourage the Japanese to attack in Asia since that would make life even more difficult for the British and tend to distract the U.S. from getting involved in Europe. The U.S. would make a Japanese withdrawal from the Tripartite Pact a condition in negotiations with Japan in the months to come, which the Japanese saw as yet more proof that America planned in due course to attack them.

THE RUSSO-JAPANESE PACT

The next major Japanese diplomatic deal was a huge surprise to the rest of the world and to many in the Japanese government: a Neutrality Pact with the Soviet Union agreed in Moscow on April 13, 1941. Although Japanese policy had been moving toward reducing tension with the Soviets for some time, saying so in public was another matter, and in fact the deal was negotiated on his own authority by Japanese Foreign Minister Matsuoka Yosuke. It did not mean that the Japanese and Soviets now liked or trusted each other, but it was an arrangement that suited both. Soviet leader Joseph Stalin (1879–1953) wanted to be free to shift forces from East Asia to Europe in case of an attack by Germany, which he was now beginning to fear. The Japanese thought a diplomatic arrangement with the Soviets was necessary for quite the opposite reason. They believed that Hitler would not attack Stalin and keep him busy in Europe. Whatever the motives, it crossed out one worry for the Japanese and made their proposed strike to the south yet more likely.

3. ATLANTIC CONFRONTATION

Sharing intelligence was not the only way in which the United States was helping Britain during 1941. Roosevelt realized that there was not much point in

Blueprint for the Future

In August 1941 President Roosevelt and British Prime Minister Churchill met at Argentia Bay in Newfoundland, one of the U.S. bases that had been established by the Destroyers-for-Bases deal almost a year before. The subjects they secretly discussed included how to stand up to Japan, what help should be sent to the Soviet Union, the Battle of the Atlantic being waged against the German U-boat menace, and many other matters of pressing mutual concern. But the conference is best remembered for a public declaration, the Atlantic Charter, which would soon in effect be a statement of America's war aims.

The Atlantic Charter affirmed American and British support for the right of people everywhere to live in democratic countries with free elections and to live peacefully with their neighbors, though it did not say how these worthwhile objectives were to be achieved. Nevertheless, the Atlantic Charter did set out at least in theory the sort of objectives the U.S. would consider fighting for, a vital step in preparing the nation for the possibility of war.

Destroyers and U-boats

By early September 1941 the U.S. Navy had already started fighting in the Atlantic theater of war. On the fourth the destroyer *Greer* was attacked by a U-boat and struck back with depth charges. Neither ship was damaged. The government publicized the incident as an example of German aggression, but that was not really true. The *Greer* had been brought into action by a sighting report from a British aircraft, and the German captain had thought he was attacking a British ship. On the eleventh the president announced that U.S. warships would now "shoot on sight" in areas "the protection of which is necessary to American defense." Later in the month American ships joined the escorts of some of the convoys sailing from Canada to Britain for part of their routes.

Roosevelt was not telling the American people the whole truth, but it is not the case that he was recklessly provoking the Germans into starting a war. The president knew from broken codes that Hitler had ordered his U-boats to avoid attacking American ships, and he was therefore able to take a tough line in the knowledge that it was safe to do so because Hitler did not want war. Code-breaking information was also used to avoid clashes rather than seek them, which would also have been possible had Roosevelt wanted war.

U-boats at harbor in the Baltic in 1940. By then they were sinking a huge tonnage in the Atlantic and would soon clash with U.S. warships.

Even so, with U.S. Navy ships in the western half of the Atlantic now doing everything that British and Canadian ones were doing, further confrontations inevitably followed. In mid-October the *U.S.S. Kearny* was torpedoed while it was escorting a British convoy. Eleven Navy men died. On October 31 the destroyer *Reuben James* was sunk with 115 dead. Few Americans realized that their forces had already been committed so deeply to the fighting, but the president used the shock that followed these losses to persuade Congress to repeal other provisions of the neutrality laws. American cargo ships could now be armed and were allowed to enter war zones. Even at this late stage these measures met with fierce domestic opposition.

producing Lend-Lease weapons for the British only for the Germans to sink the ships carrying them across the Atlantic. Through the year the U.S. Navy therefore took a more and more active role alongside the British and Canadians in fighting the German U-boats. Just how far from the old ideas of neutrality American practices went was not always made clear to the American people. American ships were hit and sailors were killed in combat operations months before the United States went to war.

The first important steps came in April, when President Roosevelt announced that 10 ex-Coast Guard ships were to be transferred to the British, that damaged British warships could be repaired in American shipyards, and that British warships generally could refuel in the United States. Next America and the exiled Danish government announced that the

United States would now be responsible for the defense of Greenland; air bases and other installations useful in the Atlantic campaign were quickly built there.

When the European war began, the United States had established a Pan-American Neutrality Zone off the North and South American coasts, which warships of non-American countries were warned not to enter. (Canada was a British dominion, so British and Canadian warships counted as "American" for this purpose.) In April 1941 Roosevelt ordered that in the North Atlantic this zone be extended to cover the area between the U.S. coast and the line of longitude 25 degrees west, roughly halfway across the ocean. Foreign warships—which meant German U-boats—inside this zone were liable to attack from U.S. Navy ships. The president described this and other moves as steps to enhance Western Hemisphere defense to make it difficult for the isolationists to protest against them.

On May 21 the American cargo ship *Robin Moor* was sunk by a U-boat, which helped Roosevelt make further moves in the following weeks. On July 7 a U.S. Marine garrison replaced the British troops who had been based in Iceland since mid-1940, after the Icelandic government had been "persuaded" to ask for American protection, and the border of the North Atlantic Neutrality Zone was extended farther east still to include the whole of that island. The pretext of supplying the Iceland garrison was next used to allow U.S. Navy ships to escort

German Panzer divisions leave a trail of devastation in their wake as they rumble eastward through Russia in summer 1941.

vessels of any nationality sailing to and from Iceland if they "happened" to join convoys on their way to the Marines.

OPERATION BARBAROSSA

On June 22, 1941, the world was stunned by yet another new development in the war: Operation Barbarossa, the Nazi invasion of the Soviet Union. Within days President Roosevelt announced that he would send Lend-Lease supplies to the Soviets. This was a bold act of leadership by the president. Opinion polls that summer and debates in Congress showed that the American people were still opposed to joining the war. Another president, even with the same aims in mind as Roosevelt, might have decided that helping the Soviet communists was just too much. Whether American help did the Soviets much good at first is doubtful, but it would certainly be significant and play a large part in defeating Germany's armies later in the war.

4. JAPAN'S FATEFUL DECISION

When Barbarossa began, Japan briefly considered abandoning its newly negotiated Neutrality Pact with the Soviets, but soon discarded this possibility. On July 2 a Japanese government meeting decided to seize new bases in southern Indochina as a stepping stone to further advances to the south, even if that meant going to war. At the same time, attempts to negotiate an acceptable deal with the Americans were to continue. Once again the Japanese did not see this as making an irrevocable decision to follow an aggressive plan. Even the most warlike of them had not committed themselves entirely, but crucially the United States found out what the meeting had discussed and arrived at a different conclusion.

Japanese diplomats abroad were sent a briefing outlining the plans agreed at the meeting, and this message was decoded and read in Washington. The United States

Codes and Code-breaking

Every country that fought in World War II made considerable efforts both before and during the conflict to read the coded radio messages their enemies used to communicate with their armed forces and their diplomats in other countries. Some of every country's codes were broken for at least some of the time, but in general the Americans and the British were the most successful in reading other countries' messages and in keeping their own secure. This had important effects in the dramatic period of increasing U.S. involvement in the struggle that preceded Pearl Harbor.

The most important American code-breaking successes were with Japanese codes. From September 1940 up to the time of the attack on Pearl Harbor at the end of 1941 and beyond, the U.S. Army's Signal Intelligence Service was able to read messages sent in the main Japanese diplomatic code. Other Japanese codes were also broken by both Army and Navy departments at various times. Information from Japanese codes could also shed light on German plans. Messages sent home by the Japanese ambassador in Berlin regularly included information that he had been given secretly by the Germans. The British were given copies of the Japanese code machines the U.S. Army had made, and during 1940 the U.S., British, and Dutch agreed to share intelligence information they gained by these and other means about the Japanese.

In the period before December 1941 the British had far more success with German codes than did the Americans. From the American point of view the most important aspect of this was that from the early summer of 1941 Britain was able to read the codes used by Germany's Atlantic U-boats and shared that information with the U.S. The U.S. therefore knew that Hitler had instructed his U-boats to avoid attacking American ships and also often knew roughly where U-boats were.

Code-breaking did not tell the American policymakers everything they wanted to know. Details of military plans and orders, like those for the Pearl Harbor attack, were often not sent out on radio at all but delivered in other ways that could not be intercepted. Many enemy signals could not be decoded (for example, the main Japanese Navy code was not being broken in December 1941, though it had been earlier and would be again later), and breaking the signals that could be read might take so much time that they would be out of date before they could be acted on. Finally, code-breaking and other information had to be brought together, interpreted correctly, and distributed to those who needed to know. In 1941 the U.S. had several organizations trying to do parts of this job but no overall system to coordinate operations and ensure that the information got to the right place at the right time.

---

decided that Japan had passed the point of no return and that this meant war within a few weeks. The administration decided that while America would not start a war with Japan, the United States should bring to bear the strongest economic pressure it could as soon as possible. That would be the only possible way to persuade the Japanese to avoid war. If war came, then any damage done to Japan's war effort in the meantime would be worthwhile. This tough new

U.S. line surprised the Japanese and strengthened the position of the more aggressive Japanese leaders. They saw it as further proof that the United States did not take negotiations seriously and intended to crush Japan. The only answer to that was war

THE U.S. EMBARGO BITES
In mid-July the Japanese forced the French authorities to agree to accept Japanese troops in southern Indochina, and the sol-

diers moved in later in the month. On July 26 the Americans and British, followed a few days later by the Dutch in the East Indies, froze all Japanese assets in their respective countries. On August 1 the president banned all exports of aviation fuel to Japan. Together these measures cut off three-quarters of Japan's foreign trade and 90 percent of its oil supplies. Japan had enough oil stockpiled for about two years of fighting, but day by day the generals and admirals could see this supply being used up. If there was going to be war, the sooner the better for the Japanese.

President Roosevelt and his advisers knew how hostile these measures would appear to Japan and were well aware that they risked war. They also believed that the continuing Japanese attempts to negotiate were not sincere, and therefore they did not try as hard

•

"Pull out of Indochina now and China later..."

•

as they might have to make them succeed. One of the reasons for this was also that Secretary of State Cordell Hull (1871–1955) in particular did not believe that Prime Minister Konoe, whom he recognized as one of the more moderate Japanese leaders, would be able to make any agreement that would be respected by the militants in the Japanese army and navy. On September 2 the Americans therefore rejected a Japanese proposal for a summit meeting between Konoe and President Roosevelt.

BREAKDOWN WITH JAPAN
On September 6 the Japanese government and armed forces held a formal meeting with Emperor Hirohito (1901–1989) to outline future policies. Japan's objectives remained unchanged, and attempts to make a deal with the United States were to continue. But that was not all. The army and navy were now instructed to make final preparations for war and to be

ready by the end of October. Early October was set as the deadline for the decision between peace and war to be made. Remarkably, the emperor broke with tradition and spoke at the meeting, making it clear that he did not want war. The army and navy were surprised and im-

General Tojo Hideki, who took over as Japan's prime minister in October 1941. He was determined to force the issue of war or peace.

pressed by how seriously the emperor took the situation, but did not change their minds. Hirohito would not speak out again in this way until August 1945, when his intervention finally persuaded his government and armed forces to bring an end to the war that they had so rashly begun.

When the deadline came in October, the Japanese were still uncertain. Prince Konoe resigned as prime minister and was replaced by General Tojo Hideki (1884–1948). In later years Tojo was

described by American leaders as an unashamed warmonger, and he was executed for war crimes by the Allies after the war was over. However, this picture was not entirely true. He was well aware that the Japanese had probably bitten off more than they could chew in China, even if they did not have to fight other countries as well, and he sincerely wanted to make some sort of deal that would avoid war with the United States. But he was also equally determined to act. In his mind Japan had been dithering for months, while the situation went from bad to worse. Japan still had a fighting chance but must take it immediately if there was no possibility of a deal.

Negotiations of a sort continued through November but never came close to succeeding. The code-breaking information available to Roosevelt and his team once again helped convince them that the Japanese did not mean to reach agreement. They knew that the Japanese ambassador in Washington, Admiral Nomura Kichisaburo, was not accurately passing on what his government told him or accurately relaying back what the Americans said in reply. This was probably merely because of incompetence and misunderstanding, but the American leadership saw it as deviousness and dishonesty on the Japanese side.

On their side the Japanese thought it was the Americans who were playing games by offering terms that they knew would be unacceptable. America's last word in the talks was delivered to the Japanese on November 27. In effect it said, "Pull out of Indochina now and China itself later, and we will let you buy oil again." No Japanese government could agree to this; on November 29 they decided on war. The U.S. had long since abandoned any real hope of peace, and at the same time as sending this proposal to the Japanese the administration had a war warning sent to commanders in the Pacific.

JAPAN'S WAR PLAN

Japanese strategy was simple. Their forces would quickly capture the British and Dutch colonies in south Asia with their vast oil, tin, rubber, and other resources. The American presence in the Philippines was a threat on the flanks of this advance, so those islands would be captured, too. To ensure that the U.S. Navy did not interfere strongly in any of this, it would be neutralized in a surprise attack on its base in Hawaii in the first minutes of the war. Once Japan had grabbed this new empire, it would have the resources it so desperately needed and would fortify a formidable defensive perimeter around

them. The United States was soft and decadent, and would make peace rather than consider the sacrifices necessary to recover what it had lost.

Crowds gather in Times Square in front of the New York Times *building as the grim news from the Pacific comes in, December 7, 1941.*

A FATAL MISCALCULATION

The attack on Pearl Harbor was Japan's worst mistake, though it did not look that way by midday on December 7 in Hawaii, with eight U.S. Navy battleships out of action after the Japanese air-

The first draft of FDR's message to Congress on December 7, 1941, urging a declaration of war on Japan in response to Pearl Harbor.

craft carriers had struck. In reality there was hardly anything the Japanese could have done that would have made Americans more determined to fight and to fight on until victory. More than a year before, the Japanese fleet commander, Admiral Yamamoto Isoroku (1884–1943), who had devised the Pearl Harbor attack, had prophesied that he could give the United States and its allies a very hard time for six months, but then Japan would gradually be crushed. He was exactly right.

One possible plan of action for Japan would have been to attack only the British and Dutch colonies in Malaysia and the East Indies and not to strike at the Philippines or Hawaii. This could have given the U.S. government a problem. Although such a move would clearly have been a threat to important American interests, could the United States have gone to war to protect other countries' colonies? It might well have been best for Japan to have tried this strategy, but the arrogance of most of the Japanese admirals and generals was so great that they did not think it essential to do everything possible to keep America out of the war.

DID ROOSEVELT KNOW IN ADVANCE?

The fact that in the days before the attack on Pearl Harbor President Roosevelt and his cabinet worried that the Japanese might only attack Malaysia and the East Indies is one of the best pieces of evidence on another controversial matter. As more evidence about code-breaking and intelligence information in the last days of 1941 came to light after 1945, some of it seemed to suggest that the president and his staff had real knowledge of the coming attack on Pearl Harbor and did nothing about it so that they would get their way and drag America into war.

Detailed studies of the records have proved to most historians' satisfaction that this is untrue, though some die-hard conspiracy theorists still put forward a related claim, that the British knew and did not send a warning so that America would be forced to fight as Britain's ally. This is almost certainly another fiction.

DECLARATIONS OF WAR

On December 8, the day after the attack on Pearl Harbor, the United States declared war on Japan. America First and isolationism had died overnight. Only one representative voted against the motion in Congress, Jeannette Rankin of Montana,

President Roosevelt signs the declaration of war against Japan, December 10, 1941. Germany and Italy then declared war on the U.S.

who had also voted against entering World War I in 1917. On December 11 Germany declared war on the United States. Congress replied with a U.S. declaration of war on Germany. Congress also voted that American servicemen could be sent to fight in any part of the world and passed a measure extending the term of men drafted under the Selective Service Act until six months after the end of the war, whenever that would be. Without Hitler's decision to

declare war the United States might well not have become directly involved in the European war. Like the Japanese, Hitler underrated American power, and like them, he and his country paid a heavy price for this mistake.

SEE ALSO

◆ Volume 6, Chapter 2, The Victory of Authoritarianism

◆ Volume 6, Chapter 3, Foreign Policy

◆ Volume 6, Chapter 5, The United States in World War II

5

THE UNITED STATES IN WORLD WAR II

Although the United States was forced into World War II by the Japanese strike on Pearl Harbor on December 7, 1941, it had in fact been preparing for belligerency since 1939, when war broke out in Europe. The U.S. had also been materially aiding its future Allies in their battle against German, Italian, and Japanese aggression well before the fateful attack.

WAR'S FIRST CASUALTY

AMERICA FIRST COMMITTEE

Powerful imagery in an America First Committee poster. It reflected widespread revulsion at the idea of U.S. involvement in overseas wars.

In the years immediately prior to World War II the administration of President Franklin D. Roosevelt strove to protect the United States against the rising tide of militarism and aggression, which centered on Adolf Hitler's Nazi Germany, Benito Mussolini's fascist Italy, and nationalistic Japan. The Neutrality Act of 1937 sought to prevent the country from becoming embroiled in any future conflict (see Chapter 3, "Foreign Policy," and Chapter 4, "The Road to War").

Under its provisions the president could proclaim the existence of a "state of war" and use the act's provisions to preserve U.S. neutrality. For example, the act permitted Roosevelt to ban the sale of arms or the issuing of extended financial credits to any belligerent state; U.S. merchant ships could be stopped from carrying war goods; citizens could be barred from traveling on belligerent vessels; and U.S. vessels could be prevented from being armed. In effect, the act potentially curtailed the country's cherished right to engage in international free trade if a state of war existed somewhere in the world.

Roosevelt's worked to put in place a rearmament program designed to protect both the continental United States and its maritime trade. It centered on the Naval Act of 1938. The act called for a long-term expansion of the U.S. Navy, which was already second in size only to the powerful British navy. It was chiefly a response to the rearmaments program of Nazi Germany and Japan's invasion of China the previous year. The latter

Republican candidate Wendell Willkie in the 1940 presidential campaign. He broadly supported FDR's policy of aid for the Allies.

aggression was seen as a direct threat to U.S. maritime interests in and around the Pacific.

1. ROOSEVELT'S BALANCING ACT

Roosevelt believed that the two acts would reassure the wider U.S. public, which continued to back the country's post-World War I isolationist position, but both he and his advisers saw that European fascism and Japanese nationalism were aggressive and expansionist forces. This was reinforced by the Nazi invasion of Poland on September 1, 1939, which precipitated British and French declarations of war against Nazi Germany and heralded

In September 1939 New Yorkers read the grim news telling them that the Nazis have invaded Poland; World War II has begun.

A message to Americans that Great Britain's fight for survival against the Nazis in 1940 was not something they could ignore.

World War II. The U.S. administration may have wished for the defeat of the aggressor, but there was little popular support for direct involvement. However, Roosevelt won one concession—in November the Neutrality Act was amended to allow the sale of munitions to the Allies.

Matters deteriorated rapidly. In the first half of 1940 the German Blitzkrieg (lightning war) offensives brought much of Western Europe under Nazi control, and Great Britain was left fighting for its life. The United States seemed even less secure, particularly since there were fears that the powerful British fleet might fall into the hands of Nazi

Germany, and moves were made to bolster the nation's defenses. The armaments program was increased, and the Revenue Act increased tax rates and reduced exemptions to partly cover the cost. The Reconstruction Finance Corporation, a body established under the New Deal, was ordered to stockpile vital raw materials and finance the building of plants to produce war goods.

In May 1940 Roosevelt created the National Defense Advisory Committee (NDAC) of leading industrialists to bring order to the purchase and distribution of scarce raw materials and skilled labor. In June National Guard units were alerted to prepare for federal service in the U.S. Army, and in September Congress backed a measure to install peacetime conscription for the first time in the nation's history.

Preparing for Conflict
In January 1941 greater emphasis was placed on rearmament. On the seventh the powerful Office of Emergency Management took over from the NDAC. Its chief body was the Office of Production Management (OPM) under William Knudsen of General Motors. Knudsen had wide-ranging powers—to increase production, to oversee the flow of raw materials into military and essential civilian services, to supervise the supply of labor, and to prioritize defense purchases. In March the National Defense

Mediation Board, part of the OPM, was empowered to arbitrate labor disputes in vital sectors of the economy. Other government committees followed: the Office of Price Administration in April and the Supply, Priorities, and Allocation Board in August. There was also increasing evidence that FDR was willing to directly aid those fighting Nazi Germany. In September 50 old destroyers were swapped with Britain in exchange for 99-year leases on eight British bases. Then in March 1941 Congress passed bill H.R.1776, better known as the Lend–Lease Bill. It allowed Roosevelt to sell, exchange, "lend, lease, or otherwise dispose of" any defense materials (weapons, transport,

•

"...lend, lease, or otherwise dispose of..."

•

food, repair services, training, and information) to any country whose defense he saw as "vital to the defense of the United States."

Against this background of the country's movement to war-preparedness the business of domestic politics continued. In 1940 Roosevelt was reelected for a third term, and he viewed his victory as an endorsement of his policy of supporting the Allies materially, but he had to move warily. Some influential figures argued against involvement and backed continued isolation. For example, historian Charles A. Beard argued that intervention would harm U.S. interests without bringing any major benefit to the

British leader Winston Churchill and FDR meeting in Newfoundland in August 1941, which resulted in the far-sighted Atlantic Charter.

blueprint for the conduct of world affairs after the war had been won. The document was wide-ranging. Among its provisions it promised the disarmament of the aggressors and that the victors did not desire territorial gains from the conflict, that national boundaries would remain unaltered barring the "freely expressed wishes of the people concerned," and that the right of self-government would be restored. It proved a powerful document against the aggressors. By January 1942 the charter was supported by 24 nations, ultimately 45, and it would provide the basis for the creation of the postwar United Nations. However, in mid-1941 the United States was mainly

wider world. Conversely, the Committee to Defend America by Aiding the Allies argued that democracy in the New World was best protected by the United States' defending democracy in the Old World.

Undeclared War with Germany

In June 1941 the United States froze German assets and closed its consulates, although diplomatic relations had in fact been frozen for months. The same month, following the Nazi invasion of the Soviet Union on the 22nd, Lend–Lease was extended to the latter. In July U.S. troops landed in Iceland to bolster the strategically important North Atlantic island's garrison, and conscription was extended.

Then in August Roosevelt met Britain's war leader, Winston Churchill (1874–1965), in New-

An aerial view of Philadelphia Navy yard, where obsolete U.S. destroyers were being refitted ready for transfer to Britain's Royal Navy.

foundland to discuss the war and its aftermath. Their discussions resulted in the Atlantic Charter, a

preoccupied with its growing involvement in the ongoing war rather than any future peace.

By the end of the year U.S. aircraft were patrolling the western Atlantic, and three U.S. warships had been attacked by German submarines with loss of life. In response, the last vestiges of the Neutrality Act were swept away. Congress agreed to the arming of merchant ships. War zones prohibited to U.S. ships were amended to permit such vessels to carry supplies to Britain and its empire. By late 1941 U.S. neutrality was in effect over.

Japan Strikes

Although many Americans expected Nazi Germany to precipitate U.S. entry into the conflict, it was in fact Japan that brought about direct U.S. involvement. During the fall of 1941 all diplomatic efforts to persuade Japan to halt its aggression in China and Southeast Asia came to nothing. On December 6 Roosevelt gave a public address calling on Japan's Emperor Hirohito to intervene personally. The Japanese response, planned for some time, came the next day. Pearl Harbor, the chief U.S. naval base in the Pacific, was attacked by carrier-borne aircraft of the Imperial Japanese Navy.

Congress recognized the existence of a state of war with Japan on December 8. Germany and Italy declared war on the United States shortly thereafter, and the Roosevelt administration responded in kind.

2. THE NATION AT WAR

The declarations of war led to a huge expansion of the U.S. armed forces. The basis for this was the Selective Service Act of 1940, which was administered by local draft boards. Prior to Pearl Harbor few eligible men had been drafted, but those who had were held in service for six months beyond the original one-year period. After December 7, 1941, all men between 18 and 65 had to register under the draft scheme. Only those between 20 and 45 were called up, and even some of them were exempted because of their marital status or specialized work skills.

In June 1942 Congress increased the allowance given to the dependents of servicemen, thereby reducing the number of

The Attack on Pearl Harbor

Shortly before 8:00 A.M. on Sunday, December 7, 1941, the inhabitants of the U.S. naval base at Pearl Harbor woke up to a shattering onslaught by Japanese aircraft. After two waves of bombing and aerial torpedo attacks the harbor was a site of terrible carnage—eight battleships, three cruisers, three destroyers, and four other craft sunk or wrecked. Almost 200 planes were also lost, along with the lives of 2,403 men. It was one of the greatest military setbacks in American history.

deferments. Volunteering was ended the following December, and in 1943 the call-up age was lowered to 18, while occupational deferments were reduced. Between 1942 and 1943 the number of women in the armed forces also rose dramatically, reaching a figure of some 300,000. All were volunteers, not draftees, and their service freed an equal number of men for more combat-oriented roles.

The total number of U.S. men who served in the armed forces during World War II was in excess of 16 million. Total casualties amounted to nearly 900,000; of those, 292,000 were killed and another 671,000 were wounded in battle.

The grim sight at Pearl Harbor on December 7, 1941, after Japanese planes had launched a devastating attack on the Pacific Fleet.

THE WAR ECONOMY

Pearl Harbor also prompted a government-sponsored wholesale transformation of the U.S. economy as military production became of overwhelming importance. It was essential to boost the output of raw materials and expand the manufacturing base that turned them into weapons, munitions, and other war-related goods. Higher market prices for raw materials, due to increased demand coupled with government subsidies, helped producers of such strategic raw materials as copper, lead, and zinc raise their output. Aluminum and steel production also rose, and a new synthetic rubber industry was started from scratch.

At the center of this activity were various government bodies, especially the Defense Plan Corporation (DFC). Among the DFC's many activities it let contracts for building 2,000 industrial plants. The "Big Inch" pipeline, built to take pressure off the railroads created by the in-creased supply of oil, the pipeline ran from Texas to the New York–Philadelphia area, a distance of some 1,250 miles, and was constructed in 1942 and 1943. It could carry 335,000 barrels of oil every day.

The rapid expansion of the economy created labor problems for the wartime administration. In 1940 the workforce totaled some 53 million workers, of whom some five to eight million were unemployed. Initially there was a shortage of skilled workers, in part because the Great Depression had reduced the need for skilled labor and thus undermined the normal incentives to acquire such skills. Some attempts were made to boost skill levels, but the government placed greater emphasis on mass production. The unskilled and semiskilled carried out the mundane tasks, while the skilled were directed to those areas where their trades were essential.

Uncle Sam rolls up his sleeves as the United States goes to war. Initially volunteers were sought, but the draft quickly became the norm.

The Demand for Labor

By late 1942 another labor problem had arisen—a shortfall in the number of workers available. The War Manpower Commission (WMC) was empowered to coordinate the allocation of men (and women) to the armed forces, merchant marine, war industries, and some civilian production as well as into farming, forestry, mines, and railroads. The next year, building on the efforts of the WMC, the United States Employment Service was given wide powers to keep workers in war production and exert pressure to force others into such jobs. The working week was lengthened, more women were employed, and 14- to 17-year-olds were allowed to work.

Navy recruits enlist in New York in the aftermath of Japan's sneak attack on Pearl Harbor. There was a burning desire for revenge.

A contemporary illustration showing America's industrial and military supplies to overseas positions in millions of dollars.

Science was also harnessed in the country's war effort. In 1941 the Office of Scientific Research and Development was created to act as a conduit between the wider scientific community, the government, and the armed forces. The most startling advance was in atomic fission, which in the period from 1940 to 1945 evolved from the realm of theory into the atomic bomb. The first bomb was tested at Los Alamos, New Mexico, in July 1945, and two were used in earnest the following month, when the Japanese cities of Hiroshima and Nagasaki were flattened. Other scientific advances occurred in

radar, antisubmarine warfare, navigation, and munitions. In the realm of medicine the mass production of penicillin to treat infected wounds was perfected, and the pesticide DDT was harnessed to combat malaria.

The War Production Board
In January 1942 the OPM, which had overseen the country's rearmament and preparedness program, was replaced by the War Production Board (WPB) under Donald M. Nelson, head of the Sears, Roebuck company. The WPB was tasked with forging and running war production. Its role was strengthened by the Second War Powers Act of March 1942, which gave the agency the right to use resources and industries in any way vital to defense and to prose-

cute any dissension. Many other specific bodies were allied to the WPB, each with its own area of responsibility. Among them were the Office of Defense Transportation, the Oil Administration, the War Labor Board, the War Manpower Commission, and the Office of Economic Stabilization. The government's aim was to forge an effective and efficient war economy at top speed. The various bodies had powers of coercion, but preferred to work in tandem with industry and the representatives of labor.

AN ECONOMY IN OVERDRIVE
How effective were these measures? There were tensions and bottlenecks, but they were overshadowed by the success of the various government agencies. Output almost doubled between 1940 and 1945, chiefly because of the increased use of industrial capacity, the further development of mass-production techniques, and longer working hours. A good example of productivity was supplied by the aviation industry.

•

"We made 300,000 airplanes, more than 15 million rifles..."

•

The administration aimed to produce 50,000 aircraft per year. The target was nearly reached in 1942 (47,653). In the following year more than 85,000 were produced, a figure that rose to 95,237 in 1944.

Shipping also showed a dramatic increase. By 1943 more than one million tons of shipping came

The final joint being welded in the famous "Big Inch" pipline linking Texas oil fields and Pennyslvania refineries, April 19, 1943.

off the slipways each month. This was partly due to the production of standardized, prefabricated freighters, known as "Liberty ships." The already large Navy also underwent expansion. In 1941 it comprised 1,200 warships of all types; by 1945 the figure was 61,045 vessels. Construction times for ships dropped dramatically. A prewar aircraft carrier took two to three years to build; during the war the figure fell to just over 12 months. The prodigious output was summed up by the veteran financier and government adviser Bernard Baruch (1870–1965): "We made 300,000 airplanes, more than 15 million rifles and carbines, 319,000 pieces of field artillery, 86,000 tanks, 64,500 landing craft, 32 million tons of merchant shipping."

Rising Prices and Wages

Such an unprecedented increase in economic activity had implications for prices and wages. Between 1939 and late 1945 wholesale prices rose by 37.2 percent. Although high, this was considerably lower than during World War I, when the figure was 100 percent.

However, price rises were offset by wage increases. Between 1939 and 1945 real wages rose by 44.1 percent. This was accompanied by income redistribution. From 1935 to 1936 Americans

Building the Atomic Bomb

The Manhattan Project, the secret program to develop the world's first atomic weapon, accelerated in the summer of 1942. The key was to demonstrate that atomic theory had practical military applications. Research centered on creating weapons from plutonium and uranium.

American and European scientists both took part in the development, but the facilities and finances were chiefly provided by the U.S. Some $2 billion was spent, not least in the creation of several research facilities, a task overseen by Army General Leslie Groves. Chief among them were Oak Ridge, Tennessee, a center for uranium production, and Hanford, Washington, which was built to produce plutonium. Efforts to create a viable weapon from the two materials were based at Los Alamos, New

Mexico, in laboratories run by the physicist J. Robert Oppenheimer (1904–1967).

The first test of an atomic device, a plutonium-based bomb known as Fat Man, was codenamed Trinity. It took place at Alamogordo bombing range in New Mexico on July 16, 1945. There was enough plutonium available after the successful test to build a second Fat Man, but only enough uranium for a single device. Unbeknown to those at Alamogordo, the administration had already sent the only available uranium bomb, codenamed Little Boy, to the Pacific. It was dropped on the Japanese city of Hiroshima on August 6. The remaining Fat Man was unleashed against Nagasaki three days later. Destruction on a vast scale precipitated Japan's surrender and the end of World War II.

A meeting of industrial executives of the Office of Price Administration (OPA), which controlled pricing of goods.

earning between $2,000 and $5,000—the middle classes—amounted to around 16 percent of the working population, but by 1945 the figure was close to 45 percent. Some changes resulted from individuals working in higher-wage industries, but lower-skilled workers also benefited from rising wages and overtime payments. There was also an increase in the membership of labor organizations. Some 65 percent of workers in manufacturing had the protection of collective bargaining, which could also boost their earnings (see Volume 4, Chapter 6, "The Unionization of Labor").

Although workers benefited economically from the war's demands, relations with bosses and the government were not always smooth. There was resentment when the War Labor Board, founded in January 1942, introduced regulations to peg wage increases to 15 percent—the rise in the cost of living since 1939. The worst case of unrest came in 1943, when key coalminers struck, and 17.5 million man-days were lost. The government stepped in to take temporary control of the mines.

In June 1943 the Smith-Connally Act imposed strict guidelines on strike votes and authorized the government to take over strike-bound plants needed for war work. Mines were taken over in the fall, and the railroads followed in December 1943.

THE END OF THE GREAT DEPRESSION

Overall, the strengthening of the U.S. economy brought about by the demands of the war had

several beneficial implications. The worst scourges of the Great Depression—poverty, hunger, homelessness, and unemployment—largely disappeared. Incomes and living standards generally rose. However, the social and economic upheavals caused by forging a war-based economy also brought their own social problems and tensions.

On the positive side the war initially led to general greater levels of social unity as people "pulled together." The continental United States itself was untouched by fighting or air attack, and most Americans suffered little actual hardship or fear. Therefore morale generally stayed high. The death of a loved one in combat was obviously traumatic, but the United States as a whole suffered less in this respect than other combatant nations. For example, the U.S. total of under 300,000 war dead is only a small fraction of the 11 million Soviet servicemen killed, and nearly as many Soviet civilians lost their lives in the brutal war with the Nazis.

SUPPORTING THE WAR EFFORT

Most people willingly made personal sacrifices for the war effort, and they were generally borne with good cheer. Many made individual decisions to support their country at war, believing it was their patriotic duty. One civil defense spokesman caught the prevailing mood: "But the cheerful side…is that the war offers us stay-at-homes a greater chance for real service than any war in the past."

The Roosevelt administration reacted to this popular support and desire to do something tangible by channeling activities into worthwhile areas. The Office of Civilian Defense, for example, stated and restated in the media that personal sacrifices—anything from sharing car journeys to work to avoiding the hoarding of scarce goods—could significantly contribute to victory. A badge of merit, the V[ictory] Home Award, was presented to families that had conspicuously saved fuel, taken part in salvage drives, bought war

Liberty ships under construction in 1942. Applying assembly-line techniques enabled the industry to achieve record productivity.

bonds, and refrained from spreading unfounded rumors.

Decisions by individuals and families to get behind the war effort were mirrored by communal activities. In larger towns and cities neighborhoods might band together to grow vegetables in "Victory Gardens." Groups of children often scoured attics, garages, and wasteland for valuable scrap metals. Door-to-door collections were common. Propaganda stunts, such as donating an old car for recycling, were frequent. People at all levels of society could become involved, thereby demonstrating that all were making sacrifices.

People were also brought together, at least initially, because of

Building the Liberty Ships

During World War II German, Italian, and Japanese submarines sank thousands of Allied merchant vessels, threatening the flow of essential war goods and foodstuffs between the U.S. and the European and Pacific theaters of operations. Traditional shipbuilding methods were far too slow to keep pace with the scale of losses. Replacement vessels had to be built in greater numbers and in much less time.

The answer lay with the so-called Liberty ship, a mass-produced, prefabricated merchant vessel with an all-welded hull. The original design, dating from as far back as the late 1870s, was English, and the plans were adopted by the U.S. Maritime Commission in 1940. Direct control of the building program, which began the following year, was handed over to industrialist Henry Kaiser. The vessels were of a simple design that was easy to build quickly, could carry large volumes of cargo,

and could survive considerable battle damage. Sections of each Liberty ship were preconstructed to a set blueprint and then transported to a shipyard, where the various sections could be assembled in as little as 10 days. The standard vessel weighed 10,500 tons when fully laden and had a top speed of 11 knots.

The first Liberty ship, the *Patrick Henry*, was launched at Baltimore on September 27, 1941, and a total of 2,770 had been constructed by the war's end. The vast majority carried general cargo, but others had more specialized roles. Sixty-two Liberty ships were built as tankers, 36 for carrying aircraft, 24 were colliers, and 8 transported tanks. In conjunction with the effective Allied antisubmarine campaign the almost continuous stream of convoys made up of these vessels was decisive in maintaining the flow of vital supplies between the United States and the other Allied powers.

Plowing a Victory Garden on Boston Common in April 1944. Such activities gave civilians a sense of being part of the war effort.

a shared sense of immediate danger in the early stages of the war and a revulsion toward the enemy. In the first few months after the Japanese attack on Pearl Harbor invasion fears swept both the West and East Coasts. Equally, propaganda stressed the evil nature of the enemy—or their leaders.

In the case of Germany and Italy propaganda was generally directed against their dictators, Adolf Hitler (1889–1945) and Benito Mussolini (1883–1945), rather than the German and Italian people as a whole. This was partly because the U.S. administration did not wish to offend the country's sizable and politically powerful immigrant populations. But it also reflected the fact that these European populations were viewed as equals, even if they had temporarily succumbed to the false siren of fascism. This was not the case with Japan. Its leaders were

vilified as bloodthirsty warmongers and, with more than a whiff of racism, so were its citizens. This perception had a great effect on the Japanese-American minority in the United States.

THE PLIGHT OF JAPANESE-AMERICANS

Japanese-Americans suffered greatly from the widespread anti-Japanese feeling in the United States—some 130,000, two-thirds of them American citizens, were forced from their homes and interned in camps in usually desolate areas. They were particularly vulnerable. Japanese-Americans formed a relatively small and tightly knit community, were concentrated along the West Coast (thought to be threatened by invasion after Pearl Harbor), and were easily recognizable. They also lacked the political clout of the larger, more established German and Italian immigrant communities.

Issei, foreign-born Japanese who had arrived before 1924, were barred from citizenship, even

though their U.S.-born offspring, known as Nisei, were citizens—but most were too young to vote. Nor did the Japanese-Americans have much economic power—40 percent worked on small vegetable farms, while many of the remainder were employed in domestic service or owned businesses that catered to their own community.

On February 17, 1942, the administration, responding to pressure from the U.S. Army, agreed to evacuate all Japanese-Americans away from the West Coast, and two days later a zone prohibited to the community was drawn up. Initially, Japanese-Americans were free to move elsewhere in the country, and some 9,000 had relocated by March. However, the towns to which they moved began to complain. Milton Eisenhower, brother of the famous General Dwight Eisenhower and head of the government's War Relocation Authority (WRA), which was to oversee the Japanese-American community, stated:

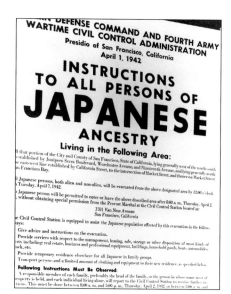

The first exclusion order against Japanese-Americans, posted in San Francisco in April 1942. Evacuees were housed in special centers.

"Violence was threatened. Japanese-Americans were arrested. Mass meetings that warned of trouble were held."

It was decided that Japanese-Americans should be settled in special WRA camps. Ten such camps, each holding up to 12,000 people, were built in several western states. Their movements were overseen by the Army, but the WRA did not expect Japanese-Americans to remain in the camps for the duration of the war. Those against whom no evidence of disloyalty could be proved were free to leave if they had found employment away from the coast, could show that they would be accepted by the new community, and informed the authorities of any change of address.

In 1943 some 17,000 met these requirements and left the camps. About 35,000, mostly

•

"Violence was threatened. Japanese-Americans were arrested."

•

Nisei, had departed by late 1944. However, six states—Arkansas, Arizona, California, Texas, Utah, and Wyoming—tried to block the arrival of Japanese-Americans by restricting their right to vote, own land, or obtain commercial licenses. Life in the camps was generally dull and monotonous, and the stresses of confinement led to sporadic outbreaks of violence. Two young Japanese-Americans were shot and killed by U.S. troops sent in to restore order to

American productive capacity is shown as a bomb aimed at the heart of both the German Swastika and the Japanese Rising Sun.

California's Camp Manzanar after a riot broke out.

By spring 1944 the administration recognized that there was no military justification for the West Coast exclusion but had to tread carefully to avoid any adverse public response to wholesale camp closures. In December the exclusion order was finally dropped, and the camps slowly began to empty. By January 20, 1945, most were closing, although 5,000 Japanese-Americans were still subject to exclusion. The camps had cost $250 million to run. The freed Japanese-Americans, of whom only 50 percent returned to the West Coast, were still subject to random acts of violence and also found that most of their farms had been confiscated, or that their leases on them had expired, or that their old jobs had disappeared.

NATIONAL UNITY
For most Americans the plight of Japanese-Americans remained unknown. Of more concern, to both government and people, was fostering a sense of a nation united in purpose. National unity was promoted by large manufac-

turers and corporations, chiefly through war-directed advertising. The availability of consumer goods fell during the conflict. Entrepreneurs switched production to war goods but continued to advertise, however. They had two reasons. First, to show the wider public that they were partaking in the war effort and, second, to build up a reservoir of public goodwill that would serve them in the likely postwar boom for consumer goods. The Office of War Information backed the advertisers' efforts, summarizing its role in wartime as being "…not to influence [the citizen] to the point of spending his money for a 'product,' but to invigorate, instruct, and inspire him as a functioning unit in his country's greatest effort."

CENSORSHIP AND DISSENT
The administration also moved to control the flow of war news to the wider public. In December

Christmas together...Have a Coca-Cola

...welcoming a fighting man home from the wars

A "feel-good" Coke advertisement, in keeping with instructions to advertisers that they should help inspire people in their war effort.

1941 Byron Price was made head of the Office of Censorship. It was permitted to examine all communications between the United States and other countries, and issued the Code of Wartime Practices to the heads of newspapers and radio stations. Among its provisions were strict guidelines on reporting troop movements, casualties, and weather patterns—information that might have been of value to an enemy. Working in parallel with Price was the Office of War Information under Elmer Davis. Founded in June 1942, its chief role was to explain the administration's war policies to the general public and to smooth the relationship between the administration and the media.

Support for the war effort, widespread and sincere though it was, was not universal, nor was it continuously at a high level across the whole of society. Perhaps inevitably as the war continued, war-weariness set in, and the high level of enthusiasm waned somewhat. With victory finally in sight, individualism reasserted itself. Sections of the population also sought to benefit directly from the war, particularly black marketeers who exploited the chronic demand for consumer goods caused by rationing.

Social tensions also arose when it was believed, usually erroneously, that certain groups were not pulling their weight. Scapegoats were found—not least in the Jewish community. Available evidence suggests that anti-Semitism grew during the war. There was a view that the Jewish community was profiteering, shirked its responsibilities, and engaged in draft-dodging. Much of this unfounded ill-will was latent or expressed in private, but there were occasional outbreaks of violence. For example, three Boston suburbs saw non-Jewish teenagers desecrate synagogues, wreck Jewish-owned store fronts, and engage in clashes with Jewish youths in mid-1943.

A NATION ON THE MOVE

While serious, black marketeering and anti-Semitism were not the chief threats to the nation's social cohesion. More significant for the fabric of society was the mobility of individuals and families brought about by the demands of the war economy. Between 1941 and 1945 some 12 million men left home to join the armed forces, while some 15 million citizens moved within the United States. People moved from rural to urban areas (and vice-versa), from south to north, and from the interior to the coasts in the east, west, and Gulf of Mexico. Some 5.4 million people left country areas, while 2.5 million made the reverse journey; some one million moved from south to north, and 600,000 in the opposite direction. The greatest migration affected the West Coast—1.4 million people moved to California alone. Such moves affected both the migrants and the communities to which they moved.

The demand for labor fueled these migrations. Although the farm population declined by 17 percent during the war, agricultural productivity rose by 25 percent, due mainly to increased mechanization and the use of chemicals, and the movement toward larger farms suited to the

Black Marketeering

Rationing and price controls helped cap the cost of living and enjoyed popular support. But side by side with the rationing ran a black market in goods that were secreted away, stolen, or somehow kept out of the regulated market. Illegal though such activities were, 20 percent of Americans interviewed for a survey stated that purchasing black-market goods was justified on occasion. Such goods included gasoline, coffee, liquor, and meat.

Ensuring a Fair Share for All

Once the U.S. economy was placed on an out-and-out war footing after Pearl Harbor, the Roosevelt administration acted swiftly to ensure that the military effort was given priority in the allocation of scarce raw materials and certain foodstuffs. Some consumer goods began to disappear from shop shelves, and civilians faced shortages of previously widely available items. To stop retailers from charging higher prices and prevent richer consumers from hoarding such goods, a fairer system of distribution was created through the use of rationing.

The system, in which certificates, coupons, and stamps were exchanged for rationed goods, was overseen by the Office of Price Administration (OPA) and administered by local boards. The OPA, initially headed by economist Leon Henderson, introduced 10 major rationing programs in 1942, and others followed. Items covered by the system included some obviously war-related products,

such as gasoline and tires. Other controlled goods included processed foods, chiefly because of the large quantities of tin needed for canning, and coffee and sugar brought in from overseas, both of which tied up valuable merchant vessels. Meats, fats, cheese, and shoes (three pairs per person per year) were also rationed.

Although most Americans accepted the need for rationing, many did purchase scarce goods for money on the black market, and an estimated $1.3 billion had been spent in such a way by 1944. However, rationing was eased as soon as victory came in sight. For example, in May 1944 meat rationing, except for certain prime cuts of beef, was ended. By the close of 1945 the vast majority of goods had been removed from the rationing program.

A soldier stands in line with civilians outside a rationing board office in New Orleans, Louisiana, in 1943.

A poster issued in June 1942 to persuade motorists to pool trips to reduce wear and tear on tires. Rubber was vital for the war effort.

end, and bombers, 8,685 in total, poured out the other. More than 42,000 people were employed.

Tension simmered between locals and the newcomers. The locals felt they were being swamped and their concerns ignored; the workers felt resented and had to put up with inadequate living conditions. One local reflected general opinion: "Before the bomber plant was built, everything was perfect here. Then came the bomber plant and this influx of riffraff—mostly Southerners. You can't be sure of these people."

Such tensions were also mirrored within migrant families. Divorce rates soared during the war, from 16 per every 100 couples who wed in 1940 to 27 per 100 by 1944. The rise was in part due to disruptions in traditional family life—many fathers were on active service, and the numbers grew when the government tightened draft deferments for fathers. Thus children were left with little contact with their fathers, and increasingly their mothers, who were engaged in war work. During the war the number of female workers rose from 14.6 million to 19.3 million, some 36 percent of the total labor force.

There were official concerns about the rise in women workers. Some feared that the safeguards relating to the conditions of women workers would be undermined by the war's demands, while others believed that working women would neglect their children. Night shifts, standing in line for rations, and the need to fit in housework around their work regimen would all take a toll on

new methods. The demand for industrial labor rose enormously, principally in war-related industries, such as iron and steel, weapons, petroleum, coal, and rubber. Again there was a process of consolidation. In 1939 businesses with more than 10,000 workers accounted for 13 percent of the total labor force; by 1944 this figure had leapt to 31 percent.

THE SOCIAL EFFECT OF WAR

These great migrations and the restructuring of the economy had wide-ranging social implications. Families had to readjust to their

new work patterns and strange surroundings, often leading to frictions between them and longer-established residents. Many families migrated to virtually new communities, so called "defense cities," which were often short of decent housing or public amenities, such as schools and sanitation. For example, Ford lighted on Willow Run, a small, mainly farming community some 25 miles from Detroit, to build a vast defense city for churning out bombers. It employed the most modern production-line techniques—parts flowed in one

Male and female workers shoulder to shoulder, turning out parts for bomber aircraft. Women became a familiar sight in such factories.

Fears of Moral Decline

Older children—juveniles—also experienced difficulties adjusting to wartime. While the crime rate among adults actually dropped during the conflict, it rose among those under 18 years of age. Commentators railed against the rise in violent crime among young males and attacked the rise in sexual promiscuity among their female counterparts. Efforts to arrest this alleged moral decline included the 1941 May Act, which permitted the closure of brothels near military bases. Nevertheless, there was an alarming increase in sexually transmitted diseases. Legislation to curb their spread included blood tests before marriage. In 1940 just 20 states had such a requirement, but by 1944 this had risen to 30. The government also backed public awareness campaigns by running thousands of clinics—in 1944 alone 560,000 people sought referral.

Prohibitionists attempted to make capital out of the social disruption and supposed moral decay. Bizarrely, they cited alcohol as the main reason behind the disaster at Pearl Harbor, stating that: "Strong drink rendered the island helpless, befuddled, off-guard, and at the mercy of the heartless Japs." Despite such lurid protestations, there was little popular support for prohibition, and politicians were lukewarm in their support when not down-right dismissive.

Unlike World War I, when there was a popular backlash against those belonging to America's immigrant groups (see Volume 1,

Liberator bombers being built at Ford's huge plant at Willow Run, Michigan. There were frictions between factory workers and locals.

working women. These were genuine concerns. Schools were so overcrowded that children were being taught for half of each day, and there was an acute shortage of childcare facilities. The administration, acting under the Lanham Act of 1940, which provided funds for war-boom communities, did establish 2,800 daycare centers, but many women did not use them, preferring to rely on relatives or neighbors.

The Nation's Women at War

Huge numbers of men served in the U.S. armed forces during the war, many of whom had been previously employed in industries vital to the country's war economy. The administration initially attempted to increase the supply of labor by drawing on the large pool of unemployed and older juveniles. However, by mid-1942 the shortfall was increasingly acute, and the body responsible for overseeing war employment, the War Manpower Commission, began to encourage women to move into traditionally male-dominated workplaces.

At first, most such women were employed in light industries, manufacturing standardized components or working on production lines, but from 1943 onward they were increasingly found in heavy industries. Despite workplace discrimination, poor childcare facilities, substandard housing, and often poor health provision, women flooded into industrial work, and the propaganda image of Rosie the Riveter became part of the national consciousness. Between 1941 and 1945 the female workforce rose from 14.6 to 19.3 million, representing some 36 percent of all who were employed. Even traditional bastions of all-male labor were recruiting women. Some 10 percent of all those working in steel plants were women, and it was a similar story with shipbuilding.

Women were also being encouraged to serve in the U.S. armed forces. On May 15, 1942, President Roosevelt authorized the creation of what became the Womens Army Corps, and on June 30 a female naval reserve was established. Eventually some 300,000 women served in the Air Ferry Command, Army, Coast Guard, Marines, and Navy as clerks, instructors, mechanics, nurses, pilots, and technicians. All served on the same terms as men, although they did not carry weapons, and some served overseas. Unlike their male counterparts, however, women in the armed forces were wholly volunteers, never draftees.

A woman metalworker in a factory near Baltimore, turning out parts for U.S. Navy aircraft. As the war went on, more and more women could be found in such heavy industries, previously a male preserve.

Patriotic Italian-Americans in New York's Little Italy celebrate the (temporary) fall of Italian dictator Mussolini in September 1943.

Chapter 2, "The United States in World War I"), the country's ethnic and cultural diversity was mostly celebrated during World War II. This was in part due to the avowedly racist policies of the enemy, but the inclusive attitude (with the notable exception of the Japanese-American community) was also supported by the Roosevelt administration.

This can be best illustrated by the treatment of the German and Italian immigrants who were not U.S. citizens (and therefore, technically, enemy aliens). At the outset of the war they were forbidden to travel without permission, could not live near war-related installations, and were not allowed to own weapons, radio receivers, or maps. However, these restrictions were relaxed as the war continued, and Germans and Italians were allowed to work in war factories if they gained the necessary clearance—and most did. The Supreme Court also ruled that resident alien status did not prevent individuals from suing for wages owed or for injuries sustained at work.

Although most Americans were treated fairly, and their civil rights were not infringed, some groups were singled out for special treatment. The freedom of speech of those thought to be pro-fascist was curtailed. Government action in such cases, though perhaps heavy-handed, was widely supported. Even defenders of civil

•

"The treason press in the United States is an integral part of the fascist offensive."

•

liberties backed Roosevelt. For example, Freda Kirchway of the liberal magazine *Nation* backed the president's stance, stating that "The treason press in the United States is an integral part of the fascist offensive."

The administration created several systems to crack down on alleged domestic subversives. The Hatch Act of 1939 imposed loyalty tests on federal employees, excluding anyone who supported the undermining of the country's war efforts. Between 1940 and 1944 some 274,000 individuals were investigated, of whom 1,180 were excluded. In 1943 the Interdepartmental Committee on Employee Investigation was formed, and among the groups it investigated were the American Communist Party, the German-American Bund, and the right-wing Silver Shirt Legion.

THE AFRICAN AMERICAN EXPERIENCE

The war had profound repercussions for African Americans, acting as a stimulus for the postwar civil rights movement. Advances in civil rights during World War II reflected the interplay between several forces—the actions and tactics of leading members and groups within the African American community; the outlook and actions of the Roosevelt administration and its agencies; and the demands placed on the United States by the war. The period saw several advances in the status of African Americans and their integration into mainstream U.S. society, but advancement provoked racially motivated violence against the community by various whites.

The greater majority of African American opinion-formers took the view that while the black community should support the United States in the war, this commitment should not be at the expense of the struggle for equality.

An official photograph from May 1942 shows how African Americans had a vital contribution to make to the war effort.

African American backing of the administration had to be matched by the administration's unambiguous support for social change. The National Association for the Advancement of Colored People (NAACP) summed up the prevailing view: "If Hitler wins, every single right we now possess and for which we have struggled here in America for three centuries will be instantaneously wiped out. If the Allies win, we shall at least have the right to continue fighting for a share of democracy for ourselves."

If African Americans were to contribute to the war effort in a meaningful way, numerous barriers would have to be over-

Civil Rights Leader

Although A. Philip Randolph was persuaded to call off his planned March on Washington, scheduled for July 1, 1941, he was to get a second chance a generation later. He joined forces with Martin Luther King, Jr., in the summer of 1963 to organize the great March on Washington, in which over 250,000 took part. It was one of the high points of the civil rights movement of the 1960s and was the occasion of King's famous "I have a dream…" speech.

come, thereby allowing them to participate in a number of war-related activities. Some changes had occurred shortly before U.S. entry into the war in December 1941. The previous summer the black activist A. Philip Randolph (1889–1979) had argued for direct action against workplace discrimination by instigating the March on Washington Movement, which planned a huge march through the nation's capital.

Among Randolph's demands was the withholding of government contracts from any company operating discriminatory hiring policies. The administration, partly fearing violence between the marchers and sections of the white population, agreed to most of Randolph's demands. Randolph called the march off. However, most African Americans looked to the NAACP as the primary agency for their advancement. The NAACP favored mainstream political and legal pressure, rather than direct confrontation.

Once the United Sates had entered the war, it became increasingly evident that to ignore African Americans as a valuable source of labor would be counterproductive. However, there was much discrimination against them in industry—many worked in poorer paid jobs, had little opportunity for advancement, and suffered workplace discrimination and segregation. FDR, prompted by the NAACP as well as Randolph, acted on June 25, 1941. He signed Executive Order 8802. It banned racial discrimination in training programs and war-related industries, and established the Fair Employment Practices Committee to enforce the order. While enforcement remained spotty, by 1944 some two million African Americans were engaged in war work.

Members of the 41st Engineers build a bridge at Fort Bragg, North Carolina, in 1942. Later in the war African Americans saw combat.

Discrimination in the Forces

African Americans also faced widespread discrimination in all branches of the U.S. armed forces at the outset of World War II. They were forbidden to enlist in the Marines or the Army Air Corps; they could serve in the Navy but only as mess men, and in the Army only in separate units commanded by white officers. No African American could hold a rank above that of the lowliest white officer in the same unit. The Army even initially turned away African-American blood donors, and although the policy was eventually changed, blood plasma was segregated on the basis of the donor's race.

The treatment of and opportunities for African Americans did improve as the war went on, chiefly because the system blatantly undervalued a reservoir of potential manpower. In 1943, for example, the Army amended its literacy requirements and established a regime to improve the educational standards of African Americans.

The following year moves were made to desegregate training camps, but with mixed success. The policy was often resented by white staffs, particularly in the South, and there were incidents of racially motivated violence. The Army finally agreed to send African Americans overseas, chiefly to Europe after the D-Day landings in June 1944. Some 50 percent of its transport corps was African American, and 22 other units saw combat before the end of the war. Units remained segregated, however, and would remain so until FDR's successor President Truman outlawed the practice in the late 1940s.

THE VICTORIOUS CONCLUSION

The war cost the United States some $321 billion, of which about 41 percent was covered by taxes. The remainder was paid for by borrowing from large financial institutions, since the administration was opposed to increasing taxes further. The country's national debt rose fivefold during the war years. Overall, however, the U.S. emerged from World War II as an economically stronger nation, one willing to take a leading role in the postwar world.

The war ended the isolationism that had dominated U.S. international politics in the 1920s and 1930s. This became clear in 1944, when Roosevelt was instrumental in establishing two bodies—the World Bank and the International Monetary Fund—to prevent a return to the economic nationalism that had helped spark World War II. In the spring of 1945 signatories of the Atlantic Charter also met and agreed to form the United Nations. The United States was one of the first to join the new body. World War II left many European nations and Japan devastated; only American economic power could repair the damage caused by the most destructive war in history.

—— SEE ALSO ——

◆ Volume 1, Chapter 2, The United States in World War I

◆ Volume 4, Chapter 6, The Unionization of Labor

◆ Volume 5, Chapter 1, Government, Industry, and Economic Policy

◆ Volume 5, Chapter 2, Equality for Some

◆ Volume 6, Chapter 3, Foreign Policy

◆ Volume 6, Chapter 4, The Road to War

◆ Volume 6, Chapter 6, The Legacy of the Depression

THE LEGACY OF THE DEPRESSION

The Great Depression was one of the most important periods in the 20th century, and the man credited with pulling the United States out of depression, Franklin D. Roosevelt, was the most towering American political figure of the century. But the precise significance of Roosevelt's New Deal was questioned by contemporaries and is still much debated by historians.

Contemporary criticism of Roosevelt's policies came from two directions (see Volume 4, Chapter 1, "Left vs. Right"). The right—the Republicans, conservative Democrats, business leaders, the privileged class from which FDR himself hailed—condemned the president and his policies for enlarging the power of the state, for overregulating the world of business, and for challenging the sanctity of the Constitution in his struggle with the Supreme Court after 1935. In the eyes of the left—Democrats in the progressive tradition, socialists and labor organizers, African American leaders, and populists like Huey Long—FDR bungled an opportunity to address serious problems at the heart of society. He failed to institute real wealth redistribution—the proportions of what parts of society had the most wealth remained the same from 1920 to 1940. He left African

A poster for the Rural Electrification Administration, which brought electric power to thousands of families for the first time.

Americans in a better position than when he came to office, but the National Association for the Advancement of Colored People (NAACP) noted, "…the millennium in race relations did not arrive under Roosevelt," though it acknowledged, "Cynics and scoffers to the contrary, the great body of Negro citizens made progress" (see Volume 5, Chapter 2, "Equality for Some").

A DECISIVE TIME

On both right and left, contemporaries were aware that they were living in significant times. The Soviet Union, Germany, Italy, and Japan had all adopted extremist politics to steer them through turbulent times. Against this background British economist John Maynard Keynes (1883–1946) expressed the fears of many people when he wrote to FDR in 1933: "You have made yourself the trustee for those in every country who seek to mend the evils of our condition by reasoned experiment within the framework of the existing social system. If you fail, rational choice will be gravely prejudiced throughout the world, leaving orthodoxy and revolution to fight it out."

FDR was aware of the historical significance of the time. He said in 1935, shortly before the 1936 election confirmed the popularity of the New Deal, "There is a mysterious cycle in human events. To some generations much is given. Of other generations much is expected. This generation of Americans has a rendezvous with destiny." Such an assessment also reflected FDR's view of himself as a president in critical times, in the tradition of George Washington, Thomas Jefferson, Abraham Lincoln, Theodore Roosevelt, and Woodrow Wilson.

PRESERVING DEMOCRACY

One of the most significant legacies of the Depression was that FDR did not fail in the task with which Keynes charged him. U.S. liberal democracy proved capable of introducing the necessary change at the necessary pace within the framework of the social system. The United States turned to neither communist revolution nor fascist dictatorship. The left-wing was relatively weak, its greatest leaders dead or deported, and unions devoting their energies to recruitment drives. On the right the American Liberty League and the fascist German-American Bund attracted little popular support beyond big businessmen and German and Italian Americans.

Fascism in Germany: Girls give the Nazi salute at a rally in 1938 to mark Germany's takeover of the Sudetenland.

The United States, like Britain, France and other western democracies, overcame the problems that might have turned it to extremism through its existing system. The New Deal maintained the nature of that system rather than radically changing it. This contrasted with the contemporary situation in large parts of Europe, where economic problems and the ultranationalism they brought in reaction supported extreme parties on the right and left. In Russia, Soviet communism had been the form of government since 1917. In the 1930s Joseph

Stalin maintained high employment and output with programs of forced labor that destroyed the traditional roots of Russian society and brought death to millions.

Although left-wing groups flourished in some European countries after the war, it was the right that emerged to dominate the continent. Mussolini's Fascist party took power in Italy in 1922; a decade later, a combination of popular support and political chic-

efficiency, stability, and discipline would lead to a better economy.

Nazi ambitions led Germany to try to expand its borders by seizing territory from its neighbors. Its invasion of Poland in September 1939 brought the outbreak of World War II in Europe (see Chapter 4, "The Road to War"). World War II in the Pacific would be the result of the rise of another right-wing, militaristic society, in Japan, where economic

investigate left-wing activity, mainly among government agencies and immigrant groups. There, again, the effectiveness of the committee was limited by the fact that there was little concrete for it to investigate.

1. THE NEW DEAL

Since FDR's death in 1945 historians have debated just how much the New Deal altered the United States. The question is complicated by the nature of the New Deal itself. At the time supporters and opponents alike stressed its revolutionary nature, summed up in the speed with which FDR introduced his new policies. A more objective analysis underlines the essential conservatism of the measures Roosevelt adopted and their continuity from those advocated by Herbert Hoover before him. Like Hoover, for example, Roosevelt remained committed to balancing the budget until 1937, when a new economic recession and rising unemployment forced him to adopt deficit spending.

THE NEW DEAL AND WORLD WAR II

Another problem for historians assessing FDR's achievements is the fact that the Depression was followed by another epochal event, World War II. The two are so closely linked that it is difficult to view the Depression except through the lens of the war.

From 1939, when fighting broke out in Europe, through the United States' entry into the war in 1941 to the victory in Japan in August 1945, the war dominated and reshaped the U.S. economy. Industrial output boomed as the economy produced war material for the Allies and then also for U.S. forces; unemployment fell; places such as the naval towns of the

Flying Fortress bombers being built in a Boeing factory in Seattle, Washington. The industrial boom during World War II makes it difficult to judge the effectiveness of the New Deal that preceded it.

anery brought Adolf Hitler to the chancellorship of Germany. Like Mussolini's, Hitler's attempts to streamline the economy—the building of the highway network, for example, and the introduction of the Volkswagen, or people's car—won the admiration of observers, including Americans, who were far removed from the right wing but who believed that

ambition led the military first to invade parts of China and then to bomb Pearl Harbor in December 1941 and bring the United States into the war (see Chapter 5, "The United States in World War II").

Militaristic and right-wing voices remained largely quiet in the United States. The House Committee for the Investigation of Un-American Activities (HUAC) was set up in May 1938 to investigate profascist activity in the tense period before the outbreak of the war. There was, however, little right-wing activity to occupy it. Under its chairman, Martin Dies, it soon changed its aim to

Pacific Northwest saw their economies transformed. But how much of this was the result of FDR's policies during the 1930s and the shape in which they had left the economy? And how much would it have happened anyway, given the worldwide demand for goods that were in short supply? There is no way of telling what the history of the United States might have been without World War II.

In his message to Congress in January 1939 Roosevelt did not propose new domestic programs. He said, "We have now passed the period of internal conflict in the launching of our program of social reform. Our full energies may now be released to invigorate the pro-cesses of recovery in order to pre-serve our reforms." But recovery came not from government policy but from the outbreak of the war. The boom that followed means that there is no way of assessing how effective the New Deal would have been in rescuing the U.S.

The Twenty-Second Amendment

FDR's unprecedented four terms in office were directly responsible for the adoption in 1951 of the Twenty-Second Amendment, which stated that no president could be elected to the office more than twice. This reflec-ted the increased importance of the president in the U.S. government after FDR's presidency. It was a safeguard against a president becoming too powerful as an individual.

economy. Although FDR's programs clearly benefited many individuals and communities, it is impossible to tell whether they alone would have kick-started the economy out of depression by stimulating spending and demand. In 1937 the new recession forced Roosevelt to accept the kind of deficit spending advocated by economist J. M. Keynes in order to stimulate the economy. Again, no one knows whether the policy would have worked without the outbreak of World War II two years later.

WHAT THE NEW DEAL DID

The achievements of the New Deal were enshrined in the whirl-wind of legislation of the First Hundred Days after Roosevelt took office in March 1933 (see Volume 2, Chapter 2, "The First Hundred Days"). In only months a Congress used to obstructing presidential aims passed 15 major laws that changed the nature of U.S. government. The agencies they created had a mixed re-ception. The Civilian Conserva-tion Corps (CCC) was widely popular, as were the Tennessee Valley Authority (TVA) and the later Social Security Act. The Works Progress Administration (WPA), on the other hand, particularly politicized branches like the Federal Theater Project (FTP), brought great criticism and suspicion from conservatives (see Volume 5, Chapter 4, "The Arts in the Depression").

What linked all the elements of the New Deal? Roosevelt himself

Some New Deal projects were less controversial than others: Few people could object to the suggestion that children should read more books.

claimed, "All of the proposals and all of the legislation since the fourth day of March have not been just a collection of haphazard schemes, but rather the orderly component parts of a connected and logical whole."

Historians since have argued about just how coherent FDR's political philosophy was. Some feel that he was a supremely pragmatic politician, changing his policies to suit the moment and readily discarding those that failed. Other commentators suggest that at least the outline of a coherent approach underlay the New Deal in its three main focuses: relief and welfare, recovery, and economic and social reform. They continue to argue, however, about what Roosevelt's

This 1936 cartoon neatly sums up the complex relations between government and business. Two businessmen bemoan FDR's policies against a backdrop of news headlines announcing record profits in various industries.

priorities were. One of the most recent commentators, U.S. historian David M. Kennedy, suggests that what underlay all FDR's policies was the idea of stability: of the financial world and banking system, of farm incomes and food prices, of employment, of welfare provision.

THE NEW DEAL AND BUSINESS

One of the most controversial aspects of the New Deal was its relation with business. Business leaders and other right-wingers attacked FDR for unprecedented government regulation of private business and accused him of moving toward socialism. In many ways, however, the situation at the end of the 1930s resembled that at the start of the decade. Roosevelt's reforms were true to the fundamental tenet of capitalism— that the means of production should remain in private hands. There was no nationalization, or public ownership, of important industries such as the railroads.

The banking reforms that FDR introduced came without the creation of new institutions. The government retained ownership of some of the power-generating dams of the TVA, but that was all.

FDR was also relatively delicate in his introduction of regulation to business. Like Hoover and others before him, he emphasized cooperation between government and business and business and labor. Many business leaders originally supported the attempt of the National Industrial Recovery Act (NIRA) to impose a system of national economic controls. Later they came to perceive the people who administered the act as being antibusiness and responded by forming the American Liberty League and making the Chamber of Commerce more antigovernment. They complained of "big government" and "labor bosses."

From 1935 to 1938 business was largely against government attempts to organize reform. FDR increasingly chafed at the opposition and in the election of 1936

launched an attack on what he called "economic royalists," the big businessmen who controlled the economy in their own favor.

The coming of World War II restored harmony to government-business relations. By the end of Roosevelt's presidency regulation had grown, labor unions had become stronger, and it was widely accepted that government had a right to express its opinion on business matters. Although many business people continued to object, others believed that government moves might actually improve business conditions by achieving stability.

SAVING CAPITALISM

Numerous historians now agree with such an interpretation. The effect of the New Deal, they say, was not to push America toward socialism but to reform the nature of capitalism in the United States; not to challenge it but to strengthen it and make it uniquely American. FDR, in this interpretation, was seeking to remove from capitalism the risk of wild swings of boom and bust like those that characterized the 1920s (see Volume 1, Chapter 5, "The Fantasy World").

As early as 1932 FDR explained how the advanced stage of capitalism in the United States required a reappraisal of values that would not leave business development to "financial Titans": "Our task now is not discovery, or exploitation of natural resources, or necessarily producing more goods. It is the soberer, less dramatic business of administering resources and plants already in hand, of seeking to reestablish foreign markets for our surplus production, of meeting the problem of underconsumption, of adjusting production to consumption, of distributing wealth and products more equitably, of adapting existing economic organizations to the service of the people.... The day of enlightened administration has come. As I see it the task of government in its relation to business is to assist the development of...an economic constitutional order."

BANKING REFORM

Among the most important measures by which FDR tried to stabilize the economy was the reform early in the New Deal of the banking system and stock exchange. The financial crisis at the end of the 1920s had its roots in the weaknesses of the financial system, and FDR was determined to prevent it from happening again. He took neither of the obvious options, however, of either trying to nationalize the banks or create a new government

bank or of allowing banks themselves to reorganize and restructure the system, driving weaker banks out of business but keeping the system in private hands.

Roosevelt left the system largely as it was. The Glass-Steagall Act of 1933 separated investment banks from commercial

•

"The day of enlightened administration has come."

•

banks, meaning that savings were no longer likely to be used for risky speculation; and it guaranteed deposits through the new Federal Deposit Insurance Corporation (FDIC). This meant that there would no longer be panics or runs on the bank as depositors rushed to get their money. The moves stabilized the banking system: Bank failures fell to fewer than 10 a year after 1933.

FDR also established the Securities and Exchange Commission

in an attempt to regularize dealings on the stock market and prevent any chance of a repetition of the Wall Street Crash of 1929. It imposed requirements for the disclosure and verification of financial information by firms trading on the stock market.

2. THE DEPRESSION AND POLITICS

The Great Depression radically altered both the larger picture of American politics and significant elements within it. It brought a new alignment of political parties that would remain in place for almost 50 years; it changed the role of the president in the system; it changed the size and nature of federal government; and it asserted the primacy of federal authority over state governments.

During the 1930s the traditional party basis of U.S. politics changed its alignment. Despite the short-lived challenge from Louisi-

The home of the Federal Reserve Board in Washington, D.C. The New Deal left the banking structure largely intact, despite criticism that the Fed had proved ineffective in the face of the Depression.

This farmer left Oklahoma for California, where he found seasonal work picking vegetables. Farmers' gratitude to the New Deal made them enthusiastic supporters of the Roosevelt coalition.

ana senator Huey Long and then the populist Unionist Party in 1936, politics remained based on the two-party system.

The Republicans were far more experienced at governing—since 1861 there had only been two Democratic presidents, Grover Cleveland from 1885 to 1889 and 1893 to 1897 and Woodrow Wilson from 1913 to 1921—but Roosevelt drove them into the political wilderness for two decades. During its dominance the Republican Party had thrown up a strong progressive movement that advocated social reform. The first Republican president, Abraham Lincoln, had been responsible for abolishing slavery in the South during the Civil War, and black voters—many Southern blacks remained disenfranchised—were traditionally Republican supporters. The Democrats, meanwhile, were associated with the deeply conservative planter classes of the South.

THE ROOSEVELT COALITION

FDR's first election in 1932 saw him win the support of a wide range of voters, from big business to labor unions to conservative Southern Democrats. By the 1936 election he had abandoned this universalist platform in favor of attacking the wealthy elite and business leaders. He appealed to a range of interest groups that became known as the Roosevelt coalition. It included America's farmers, benefiting from New Deal programs to maintain prices, and urban workers, who were often first- or second-generation Jewish or Catholic voters. FDR also attracted the overwhelming majority—up to 90 percent—of the black vote.

While the Democrats became closely associated with progressivism, welfare provision, and social reform, the Republicans were cast increasingly as a conservative party, guarding the interests

of wealth and business. Both the broad alignment and the distribution of voters remained largely constant until the administration of Ronald Reagan in the 1980s.

STATES' VS. FEDERAL RIGHTS

In the early decades of the 20th century states jealously guarded their traditional political rights. Since Reconstruction ended in 1877, the Southern states had largely maintained their own social system, based on racial discrimination and the Jim Crow laws that enshrined it. At the height of the Depression in 1932, however, many states found themselves unable to pay their bills, provide pensions or care for the sick, or fund public works programs to relieve unemployment. They were forced to turn to the federal government for funds and, in so doing, to accept its funding priorities. The federal government blocked grants to states that pursued their own priorities. In this way as much as in the establishment of centralized federal agencies, the New Deal had the effect of increasing the influence of federal government at the expense of states' rights.

When the U.S. Supreme Court dropped its opposition to Roosevelt after the 1936 election and began working with him, it reinforced the primacy of the federal government. Protesters objected to the creation of the Social Security Act on the grounds that relief and welfare were the concern of states rather than the federal government. The Court ruled in

1937 that it was the right of Congress to address problems that were "plainly national in area and dimensions." This marked a development that has not seriously been challenged since.

THE SUPREME COURT

With regard to the U.S. Supreme Court, too, the New Deal brought changes. Roosevelt's long battle with the Court began in 1935, when it began to rule some of the central acts of the New Deal unconstitutional (see Volume 4, Chapter 2, "The Supreme Court"). Frustrated, FDR threatened to pack the Court with justices who were more sympathetic to his reforms. To Republicans and many Democrats alike FDR's plan challenged the balance among the executive, represented by the president and the cabinet, the legislative, represented by the House and Senate, and the third, legal branch of government, the Supreme Court. Such a change made many people profoundly uncomfortable.

Roosevelt's plan became unnecessary when the Supreme Court had a change of heart and began to reinforce New Deal legislation. FDR was exhausted by the long struggle, which stymied government business for years, but he had won the principle. The Supreme Court has never since been at such odds with an elected government. Individual nominations for Supreme Court justices remain controversial, but the dominance of the executive and legislative has not been challenged in such a concerted way.

THE ROLE OF THE PRESIDENT

Roosevelt's dominance of Congress in the early years of the Depression and the eventual reconciliation with the Supreme Court made the president a more important factor in government, which was personalized in the figure of FDR. People felt that they knew him. Roosevelt used the radio—in particular in his series of fireside chats—to explain his policies directly to the people. He gave 27 of these radio talks between March 1933 and June 1944, carefully using homely phrases and references to "we"

and "you." They were usually broadcast on Sunday evenings, when most people were listening. FDR came across as approachable and sympathetic. His cheery affability alone marked him out from some of his predecessors, such as Calvin Coolidge, who was called "Silent Cal" for his reluctance to talk, and Herbert Hoover, who was a dull public speaker.

FDR's close relationship with the people has been echoed by many presidents who followed him. Particularly successful at this kind of public presentation have been John F. Kennedy and Lyndon B. Johnson in the 1960s, Ronald Reagan in the 1980s, and Bill Clinton in the 1990s.

THE ROLE OF GOVERNMENT

The New Deal brought with it an expansion in the size of the federal government. This was partly a reflection of the fact that it was very small at the start of the Depression. In 1933 federal expenditure, raised by taxes, was only 3 percent of the Gross National Product, the value of goods and services produced in a year; that amounted to $1.9 billion. At the end of the war in 1945 that had risen to $44.1 billion, or about 20 percent of GNP. The proportion of government expenditure to GNP remains similar in most western countries today. The states and local government spent about five times more than the federal budget in 1929; by the end of the 1930s the federal government was spending more.

It was not only the size of government that grew; so did its role in national life. As government

The president takes the wheel: FDR signed this picture of himself with secretary of the treasury Henry Morgenthau.

The expansion of government brought with it the expansion of Washington D.C. The capital was one of the few cities that boomed in the 1930s.

shaping the system. In the early decades of the 20th century U.S. politics had been characterized by a struggle between individualism, which believed that there should be no restraints on economic activity, and the mutualist tradition, which believed in the importance of social moderation of the effects of unrestrained capitalism (see Volume 1, Chapter 1, "The United States, 1865–1914"). According to individualists, economic prosperity depended on the lack of regulation such as minimum wages or maximum working

powers increased, it became the country's largest banker, through loans by the Reconstruction Finance Corporation and smaller programs. The introduction of Social Security made the government the country's largest insurance provider. The activities of the Civilian Conservation Corps broadened the already established federal role in conservation. The government also went into business itself. The TVA generated and sold hydroelectric power. The WPA meanwhile subsidized cultural activity: movies, literature, drama, and painting.

INDIVIDUALISM VS. MUTUALISM

Government was no longer simply a hands-off organization dedicated to maintaining the system; it was

Foundations for the future: New Dealer Rexford Tugwell inspects new homes being built by the Resettlement Administration at Greenbelt, Maryland.

hours—the marketplace alone would dictate prices, wages, and other aspects of economic activity.

The Depression fundamentally weakened the individualist tradition. The breadlines and Hoovervilles of 1931 and 1932 were proof that the workings of capitalism produced victims—the unemployed, the poor, the exploited. Herbert Hoover—reluctantly—and more readily Franklin Roosevelt acknowledged that government had a duty to provide for these victims in terms of unemployment insurance or old-age pensions. In a capitalist economy it was the government's role to provide a human face (see Volume 4, Chapter 5, "Welfare").

THE MIXED ECONOMY

This view was part of a broader change in the role of government. In 1936 British economist John Maynard Keynes published his highly influential book *The General Theory of Employment, Interest and Money*. Keynes explained what he saw as the relationship between government and the economy, arguing that government had a duty to intervene to regulate the workings of the business cycle. The result, which emerged in the United States and other western democracies during the Depression and World War II, is termed a mixed economy.

A mixed economy is neither completely unrestrained, like a free-market or laissez-faire economy, or centrally regulated like a planned economy. Authoritarian states like Soviet Russia or Nazi Germany ran economies in which government owned businesses or dictated the amount and type of production by setting quotas for types of agricultural and industrial output; government also controlled wages, prices, and distribution.

Americans of the early 20th century were particularly suspicious of the communist model of economic planning, which abolished private profits and thus entrepreneurship. This suspicion was one reason for the continuing resistance to government involvement in the economy.

During the Depression government involvement produced a mixed economy. While business remained in private hands, the government became involved to a degree in regulating business practice by allowing union rights and minimum wages and by imposing regulation on banking and on the stock market. There was a small amount of government ownership of business, called nationalization: the main example was the power generating activity of the TVA. Keynesianism advocated the use of monetary policy to stimulate or slow economic activity, but its most important element was arguing that governments should spend money in times of depression, going into debt to do so if necessary, to stimulate the economy.

This approach, called Keynesianism, dominated U.S. economic thought for nearly 50 years. It was also adopted in other western democracies like Great Britain, France, and postwar West Germany. It was reflected in Europe in the nationalization of industries such as mining, steel production, and airlines, and in the provision of extensive cradle-to-grave welfare provision, sometimes called the welfare state. In the United States Keynesianism went largely unchallenged until the Republican administration of Ronald Reagan from 1981 to 1989. Reagan and contemporary politicians like Margaret Thatcher in Britain questioned the whole assumption of government involvement in the economy. They questioned the welfare state by arguing that it encouraged dependence and laziness in the population, rather than energy and application. Such arguments were remarkably close echoes of those of the 1920s.

3. THE NEW DEAL AND SOCIETY

It is difficult for modern readers to understand the effect the Depression had on the American psyche. For a nation

Today, as much as in the 1930s, one of the standard criticisms of government involvement in the economy is that it is more wasteful and less efficient than private business. This 1933 cartoon shows FDR priming a pump with taxpayers' money that leaks away ineffectively.

"One Person Out of Every Ten:" By 1938, when this illustration appeared in the St. Louis Post Despatch, *Americans had learned the hard way that depression was not just a temporary phenomenon.*

accustomed to consider itself the richest in the world, pictures of starving U.S. citizens were a profound shock. The previous decade, the 1920s, had been a period of almost unbridled optimism when it seemed that the economy could grow and grow indefinitely. People could make fortunes—building businesses, speculating in real estate in Florida, or buying stocks in the booming market on Wall Street. Even the jolting shock of the Wall Street Crash did not kill off the optimistic belief that after a dramatic correction, the economy would recover and thrive once more. It took three grinding years of layoffs, evictions, and highly visible poverty to achieve that.

Never again would Americans be able to believe in limitless economic growth. Economist Lauchlin Currie wrote in 1939, "The economic crisis in America is not a temporary one. The violence of the depression following 1929 obscured for some time that a profound change of a chronic or secular nature had occurred." Currie suggested that the United States was now a mature economy, incapable of supporting the growth it had before. It was incapable, too, of maintaining full employment: hence the federal acceptance of a duty to run employment and relief programs. Government had to step in to try to maintain the economy at its existing levels and to compensate for any weakness in the structure of the private sector.

The Depression has shaped economic studies since because it increased awareness of the limits of economic growth and the fear of a repetition of a sudden worldwide slump. At every later stock-market drop, economists have asked, "Is this another depression?" Neither the depth nor the duration of the Great Depression have been equaled, but business decisions tend to be made in a more cautious framework than in, for example, the mid-1920s. Share ownership remains high, but few people are unwise enough to believe that it is a risk-free investment.

NEW INSTITUTIONS
When Roosevelt took power in 1932, he declared, "We are going to make a society in which no one is left out." If the aim of the New Deal was inclusivity for workers, poor farmers, racial minorities, and women, how well did it succeed and what lasting effects did it have?

One of the effects still visible today was in the creation of the institutions of welfare. The Social Security Act of 1935 laid the foundations of the old-age pension and unemployment insurance structures that remain largely in place. The government accepted that it had an obligation to provide for its needy and disadvantaged citizens. The extent of that obligation has been questioned by numerous administrations since, particularly those politically committed to reducing federal involvement in American life. They have repeated in various guises the assertions of Herbert Hoover around 1930 when he stated that welfare would steal people's incentive to work.

Many New Deal measures brought some of the more excluded sectors of society into the mainstream. Among them, in particular, were the poor citizens of the great urban centers. They included relatively recent poor immigrants from Europe and elsewhere; they also included many of the black Americans who had moved to the cities from the agricultural South. In the South, however, black and white sharecroppers remained bitterly poor.

WOMEN IN THE NEW DEAL
For some women the 1930s were exciting times. Female politicians and advisers, like Frances Perkins, secretary of labor, or Molly Dewson, who ran the Women's Division of the Democratic National Committee, found themselves playing an important role in federal government. Perkins was the first woman cabinet member;

other women headed New Deal agencies and were particularly influential in shaping the various relief programs of the New Deal. Part of the reason for this was the tireless influence of Eleanor Roosevelt on her husband and on the Democratic Party. Dewson once noted, "When I wanted help on some definite point, Mrs. Roosevelt gave me the opportunity to sit next to the president at dinner and the matter was settled before we finished our soup." But major credit for the advancement of women in public life also goes to FDR himself.

For ordinary women the situation was not always quite so exciting (see Volume 5, Chapter 3, "Society in the 1930s"). Many had achieved economic independence since World War I, but many of those who worked in the 1920s were among the first to lose their jobs when the Depression brought the first layoffs.

Women did benefit from New Deal programs—the Works Progress Administration employed more than 400,000, and National Recovery Administration codes gave more than four million women protection at work—but they often did so on worse terms than men. Some 25 percent of NRA codes permitted women to earn lower wages than men doing the same job, for example; women who sewed on WPA projects were paid less than half what men got on other projects for the agency. Women also lost out when it came to welfare and Social Security provisions. Neither provided directly for the millions of women who did not work outside the home; the provisions of the Social Security Act did not extend to areas of employment where large numbers of women traditionally worked, like domestic service.

THE NEW DEAL AND RACE

Race relations generally improved under Roosevelt. At the start of his presidency blacks had little to hope for from the Democratic Party or from Roosevelt himself. FDR relied on Southern Democrats for support and was reluctant to pass measures that would offend them. One of the most obvious failures was FDR's refusal to pass antilynching legislation in the 1930s. A number of New Deal agencies were accused of racial discrimination. Although the administration intended measures to be applied equally,

Virtually all the workers in this tomato-canning plant are women. They were the lucky ones: In most industries women were among the first workers to lose their jobs when the Depression struck.

local officials who implemented the policies often gave blacks less opportunity than whites or distributed welfare unequally. When the NAACP and other organizations protested against this inequality, there were moves to improve it.

Eleanor Roosevelt had a strong effect with her personal demonstrations of commitment to desegregation. Through her work with the National Youth Administration she played an important part in

broadening opportunity for young black people. She was vigilant to ensure that New Deal agencies were fair in their application of relief: "It is a question of the right to work, and the right to work should know no color lines." She made many personal gestures to show her commitment: pulling her chair into the aisle between black and white members of the segregated audience at a meeting; arranging for black singer Marian Anderson to perform at the Lincoln Memorial when the Daughters of the American Revolution refused to allow her to sing at

Constitution Hall because of her color; inviting the wives of black politicians to the White House.

Eleanor and Walter White, secretary of the NAACP, tried to get FDR to introduce antilynching legislation. She later recalled the discussion: "I remember wanting to get all-out support for the antilynching bill and removal of the poll tax, but though Franklin was in favor of both measures, they never became 'must' legislation. When I would protest, he would simply say, 'First things come first, and I can't alienate certain voters I need for measures that are more important at the moment by pushing any measures that would entail a fight.'" When legislation on both measures came before the House, Southern politicians filibustered them out of existence, though some states introduced their own laws. The number of lynchings fell from 28 in 1933 to two in 1939.

After 1934 FDR tried to ensure a fairer deal for blacks under the New Deal in agencies such as the Farm Security Administration, the Public Works Administration, and the Works Progress Administration. He introduced many African Americans to government, particularly in what the press dubbed the Black Cabinet, a group of advisers and administrators that included Mary McLeod Bethune, Robert Weaver, and William H. Hastie (see Volume 2, Chapter 6, "The Election of 1936"). A recent assessment points out that "They made New Dealers marginally more sensitive to the needs of blacks; and they made the federal government seem more comprehensible and relevant to blacks."

FDR forged a relationship between African Americans and the Democratic Party. For the first time the majority of black voters

NAACP protesters outside a 1934 conference in Washington, D.C., call for an antilynching law. FDR was sympathetic to their cause, but his reliance on Southern politicians prevented him introducing the law they wanted.

deserted the Republicans in 1934; in 1936 Roosevelt ensured that black Democrats played a visible role in the National Convention, becoming accredited delegates and making speeches. In 1940 he insisted that specific black measures, including a pledge to end discrimination in government services, were included in the Democratic platform. In both 1936 and 1940 Roosevelt won nearly 90 percent of the black vote. The proportion of

•

"I can't alienate... voters I need for measures that are more important..."

•

blacks voting Democrat has remained relatively constant since.

At the end of the New Deal much still remained to be done to improve the lot of black Americans. Many, however, believed that

things had begun to change in the United States and that the Democrats were the party most likely to make the journey with them.

4. A PERSONAL LEGACY

On April 12, 1945, Franklin Roosevelt died while having his portrait painted at his cottage at Warm Springs, Georgia. Later that day the news was announced in a short news bulletin: FLASH WASHN–FDR DEAD. For years rumors would persist that FDR died in mysterious circumstances. One outlandish theory had it that he had been poisoned by the cook of Soviet leader Joseph Stalin at the Yalta Conference in February, where FDR had met the other Allied leaders to discuss the postwar shape of Europe. Another story was that no one had seen the body and that FDR had not died at all.

Such stories reflected the disbelief of the American nation and its allies. FDR had died on the eve of victory. Within a month the Italian dictator Mussolini would be dead; the Allies were closing in from East and West on Hitler's

The Cultural Legacy

The Great Depression dominated American cultural life at the time and, thanks to numerous memorable books, artworks, photographs, and movies, is one of the periods of U.S. history with which people today are most familiar. It provided the backdrop, for example, of the long-running TV show *The Waltons* and was the setting for George Clooney's 2000 box-office hit *Oh Brother, Where Art Thou?* In the 1930s the federal government encouraged and funded the most concerted attempt ever to get writers and artists to record what was happening around them (see Volume 5, Chapter 4, "The Arts in the Depression," and Volume 5, Chapter 6, "Chroniclers of the Depression"). Under the auspices of the Federal Art Project and other government agencies visual artists actively considered what was happening in U.S. society and what it meant to be American. Other branches of the project cataloged and preserved records of early American art or preserved traditional craft forms like quilting or toy making. The *American Guide* series compiled by the Federal Writers' Project remains an authoritative source of information on regional cultural history.

The Depression also brought a highpoint in the use of photography to document history. Noted photographers were employed by various government agencies and newsmagazines to record their work. The images taken by Margaret Bourke-White and Dorothea Lange of the rural poor did much to shape contemporary Americans' reaction to the economic crisis. Today many of them remain recognizable as iconic representations of poverty and suffering.

In literature John Steinbeck wrote novels like *The Grapes of Wrath* and *Of Mice and Men* that remain highly popular today. Steinbeck portrayed with documentary precision the effects of the Depression on families in poor agricultural communities. Although critics at the time condemned him for sentimentality, Steinbeck's books are now considered 20th-century classics. In 1962 he won the prestigious Nobel Prize for literature.

Perhaps the greatest cultural effect of the Depression, however, was the changed status of the movie industry in the United States (see Volume 5, Chapter 5, "Hollywood: The Depression Years"). Hollywood had become highly popular during the 1920s, but in the 1930s the cinema became perhaps the most important and most characteristically American form of creative expression. This was partly due to the perfecting of technology in terms of both sound and color. It also reflected Hollywood's ability to provide both on-screen and in the real lives of its stars an optimistic and glamorous contrast to the misery experienced by many Americans at the time.

The cinema attracted some of the most talented people of the generation and some of the most able filmmakers of any generation. Cecil B. DeMille made the historical costume drama *Cleopatra* (1934), capturing the exotic world of ancient Egypt. German immigrant Fritz Lang made the intense dramas *Fury* (1936) and *You Only Live Once* (1937). Audiences then and now alike appreciated the genial, gently comic masterpieces of Frank Capra, who believed that moviegoers could be entertained by films that were based on the justice and honor of ordinary people in everyday life. Capra's masterpieces included *Mr. Deeds Goes to Town* and *Mr. Smith Goes to Washington*.

Musicals and other genre movies were highly popular. Choreographer Busby Berkeley became famous for huge dance routines involving dozens of showgirls, often filmed from unusual angles. Sophisticated dance team Fred Astaire and Ginger Rogers glided their way through numerous movies, including *Top Hat* (1935). For those seeking a voyeuristic thrill the gangster genre came of age in *Little Caesar* (1930), *Public Enemy* (1931), and *Scarface* (1932) and the horror genre in the original versions of what became two standard movie subjects, *Frankenstein* and *Dracula*. Walt Disney's *Snow White and the Seven Dwarfs* (1937) was the first—but by no means the last—feature-length cartoon. As if to sum up the achievements of the decade, it ended in 1939 with the release of three undisputed masterpieces: *The Wizard of Oz*, *Stagecoach*, and *Gone with the Wind*—respectively a classic musical, western, and dramatic epic.

Eleanor Roosevelt

After FDR's death Eleanor Roosevelt continued to be a high-profile presence in U.S. politics, consistently arguing that government should maintain the ideals of the New Deal. She became more interested in international affairs, particularly in overcoming injustice and racial discrimination. Harry S. Truman appointed her as a representative to the United Nations. In 1948 she played an important role in the creation of the Universal Declaration of Human Rights.

Other causes she adopted were opposition to Soviet communism and support for the creation of a Jewish state in Israel. From 1947 to 1951 she served as chairman of the UN Human Rights Commission.

Eleanor remained a powerful presence at home, too. In 1936 she began writing a syndicated daily newspaper column, "My Day," in which she expressed her commitment to human and civil rights both at home and abroad. She wrote numerous books, including *The Moral Basis of Democracy* (1940), *India and the Awakening East* (1953), and *On My Own* (1958). A champion of black civil rights, she was particularly opposed to Joseph McCarthy's witch hunt against communists in the early 1950s. In 1960 John F. Kennedy appointed her head of the President's Commission on the Status of Women. Her health was failing, however, and she could not make a full contribution to the commission's work. She died on November 7, 1962. By that time she had become a powerful and much-loved national symbol of social justice, which she believed should be universal.

Eleanor Roosevelt (left) receives an award— named for her old friend Mary MacLeod Bethune—for her civil rights work.

headquarters in Berlin. In the Pacific U.S. troops were fighting on Okinawa, the island that would enable an attack on Japan itself.

Vice president Harry S. Truman (1884–1972) was sworn in as president less than four hours after FDR's death. The next day he said, "There have been few men in all history the equal of the man into whose shoes I am stepping. I pray God I can measure up to the task." Truman's assessment of his predecessor was borne out. FDR was

the towering personality of U.S. politics in the 20th century. In 1948 and 1962 U.S. historians voted him the third-greatest president of all time, after Abraham Lincoln and George Washington; a similar poll by the *Journal of American History* in 1982 placed him second, just after Lincoln.

ROOSEVELT'S SHADOW

As president FDR cast a long shadow over his successors. He had virtually created the modern style

of presidency, with his active program of reform presented to the Congress and his use of the media to form a collusive alliance with the American public. Truman himself echoed FDR's domestic policy when he came up with the Fair Deal, a more modest program of reforms that had its roots directly in the New Deal. Dwight D. Eisenhower (1890–1969), the Allied commander who became president in 1953, disagreed with many of FDR's domestic policies

Eleanor Speaks

FDR's train, the *Ferdinand Magellan*, carried his body back to Washington, D.C., for a service in the White House and then on to his estate at Hyde Park, New York, where he was buried on April 15. The train traveled at 35 miles an hour through the Carolinas and Virginia; crowds stood through the night to catch a glimpse of it. In most places blacks and whites stood separately, a sign of the deep racial divisions that still split the country. The First Lady recalled: "I lay in my berth all night…looking out at the countryside he had loved and watching the faces of the people at stations, and even at the crossroads, who came to pay their last tribute all through the night. The only recollection I clearly have is thinking about 'The Lonesome Train,' the musical poem about Lincoln's death. I had always liked it so well—and now this was so much like it. I was truly surprised by the people along the way. I didn't expect that because I hadn't thought a thing about it. I never realized the full scope of the devotion to him until after he died—that night and after. Later I couldn't go into a subway in New York or a cab without people stopping me to say they missed the way the president used to talk to them. They'd say, 'He used to talk to me about my government.'"

but nevertheless acknowledged his great qualities of leadership: "Any president, if he is to be effective, must be able to inspire people. It is an essential quality of leadership. I have often thought how fortunate it was that the two great Allies of World War II were led by two men—Churchill and Franklin D. Roosevelt—who had that ability and used it masterfully."

For later presidents FDR would be the yardstick against which they measured themselves. This was particularly true in the 1960s, when Democrats again lived in the White House. John F. Kennedy (1917–1963) evoked FDR's memory to appeal to the coalition of voters Roosevelt had assembled—poor white immigrants, African Americans, liberal intellectuals—even though he himself was ambivalent about FDR. Kennedy's father, Joseph

Ronald Reagan's claim to be in the FDR tradition showed the enduring appeal of the whole philosophy of the New Deal.

John F. Kennedy was happy to court Roosevelt's supporters at the polls but in private was less enthusiastic about his Democratic predecessor.

Kennedy, had been FDR's ambassador in London at the start of the war and was critical of the president; for her part Eleanor Roosevelt disliked Kennedy, which might also have colored his judgment. Kennedy once complained, "When Franklin had this job, it was a cinch. He didn't have all these world problems. He had only to cope with poverty in the United States, but look what I've got."

Lyndon B. Johnson (1908–1973) made a more conscious effort to ape the Roosevelt style in his presidency from 1963 to 1969. His Great Society program was a raft of social reforms in the tradition of the New Deal. Johnson introduced important legislation on medical care, civil rights, education, housing, and the elimination of poverty. He claimed that his legislative program rivaled the New Deal, but he never gained a similar level of popularity to FDR.

Such was FDR's towering reputation that even Republican presidents appealed to it. Richard Nixon (1913–1994) quoted him on numerous occasions. In 1980 the right-wing Republican Ronald Reagan, president from 1981 to 1989, set out so deliberately to invoke FDR's legacy that reporters dubbed him Franklin Delano Reagan. He echoed FDR's words, but often took them out of context or misapplied them. He claimed,

still managed to ally himself successfully with FDR's memory. What did he gain? He suggested a link between himself and the greatest politician of the century; he somehow suggested a parallel between his own program—to cut back on federal spending and the role of the state—and the New Deal. He also made it possible for liberals to support him without seeming to go against the memory of FDR. Reagan's stance was con-

regulation and increased bureaucracy; the left attacked him for not taking the chance to do more to reform the U.S. system. In foreign policy those who believed that the United States should remain isolated from international struggles accused him of pretending he was seeking peace when he was in fact determined to lead the country into war with the Axis powers—Germany and Italy—when they were no threat to the United States (see Chapter 3, "Foreign Policy"). Some critics went so far as to accuse him of provoking the Japanese to attack Pearl Harbor in December 1941 and then ignoring intelligence warnings of the attack in order to draw the United States into the conflict. Interventionists believed, on the other hand, that the president was too slow to offer U.S. help to support the democracies of Europe. Few historians now argue that FDR could have kept the United States out of the war.

FDR meets Winston Churchill (left) and Joseph Stalin (right) at Yalta in 1945. Conservatives condemned FDR for handing Eastern Europe to the Soviet Union; conspiracy theorists accused Stalin's cook of poisoning the president.

for instance, "I looked up FDR's old platform and I discovered that it called for a restoration of states' rights and a reduction in the national budget. You know what? I'm still for that."

Reagan, however, was against the fundamentals of the New Deal. He stood for reducing welfare but

demned as a sleight of hand. Senior Democrats such as Edward Kennedy and Speaker of the House of Representatives Thomas "Tip" O'Neill were outraged by Reagan's implication that, were he alive in the 1980s, FDR would have been a Republican.

THE UPS AND DOWNS OF REPUTATION

FDR has not enjoyed an entirely positive reputation in the years since his death. The battle lines had been drawn during his presidency. The right criticized his "socialist" policies of government

In the aftermath of the war Roosevelt was criticized by conservatives for having enabled the Soviet domination of Eastern Europe and for having made possible the communist revolution that brought Mao Zedong to power in China in 1949. Republicans accused him of a "betrayal" at the Yalta conference, in which he allowed Stalin to have a free hand in Eastern Europe.

Throughout the Cold War, the period of international tension between the Communist and Western blocs from around 1945 to 1989, Roosevelt was blamed for allowing Stalin to dominate Eastern Europe. In reality he had little choice. Not only did the Soviet Red Army occupy most of the region at the end of the war; FDR was also eager to ensure that the Russians would join the United

Stalin's Dime

Soon after Roosevelt died, his name was given to schools, roads, and other public works throughout the United States. FDR's portrait has appeared on the 50-dollar savings bond, on standard issue stamps, and on the dime. The Roosevelt dime was issued in January 1946 as a tribute to the former president. It was engraved by U.S. Mint engraver John Sinnock, whose initials, JS, appeared on the edge of the finished coin. Critics of Roosevelt claimed that they stood for Joseph Stalin and symbolized how much influence FDR had yielded to the Soviet Union at the end of the war.

States in the war against Japan. Above all, he had to keep together the fragile alliance of the Allies.

Roosevelt was realistic about the limits of his own power and that of the United States. He made his case simply to an aide who objected that Roosevelt had not forced the Soviet Union to create an independent Poland after the war; instead, the Soviets agreed only to inform the Americans of their actions in the region. The aide complained, "Mr. President, this is so elastic that the Russians can stretch it all the way from Yalta to Washington without ever technically breaking it." Roosevelt replied, "I know it. But it's the best I can do for Poland at this time."

Another important legacy of Roosevelt's foreign policy was his determinedly internationalist outlook. Whereas the United

A bust of Roosevelt outside the New York City post office. FDR remains one of the most celebrated of all U.S. presidents.

States had not joined the League of Nations after World War I, it was a founder member of the United Nations in 1945, largely as a result of FDR's influence.

THE PEOPLE'S PRESIDENT

Ordinary Americans continued to look on FDR as *their* president, the man who addressed them about the concerns of government and told them what would and what would not happen. He had been president through 12 years and two great national and international crises; he had become an institution and a sign of stability not only at home but also abroad. In his Four Freedoms speech of January 1941 he laid out the goals for which the nation was fighting in the war and thereby the democratic principles he saw as underlying the U.S. system. The principles dictated U.S. politics for much of the century: Freedom of Speech, Freedom of Worship,

Freedom from Want, and Freedom from Fear. These last two further marked FDR's acceptance of the responsibility of government to provide economic security and social stability, responsibilities that remain today.

GLOSSARY

balanced budget an economic term used to describe a situation in which a government's income is enough to pay for all its expenditure. The balanced budget was an essential principle in U.S. economic policy until Roosevelt adopted deficit spending in 1937. *See also* deficit spending.

business cycle an economic term used to describe the periodic but unpredictable and inexplicable rise and fall of economic activity.

capitalism an economic system in which private individuals and companies control the production and distribution of goods and services.

communism a political doctrine advocated by Karl Marx and Friedrich Engels in the 19th century that proposes the overthrow of capitalism and its replacement by working-class rule. Communism was the official ideology of the Soviet Union and was highly feared in the United States.

deficit spending an economic approach in which a government goes into debt in order to fund its activities. Deficit spending is a central tenet of Keynesianism.

depression a deep trough in the business cycle. No other depression matched the intensity of or lasted as long as the Great Depression.

fascism a political ideology based on authoritarian rule and suppression, aggressive nationalism, and militarism.

gold standard an economic tool that used gold as the measure of a nation's currency, so that one unit of currency always bought a fixed amount of gold. It was chiefly useful in stabilizing exchange rates between currencies.

Hundred Days the name given to Roosevelt's first period as president, from March 9 to June 16, 1933, characterized by a whirl of legislative activity. It was named for the Hundred Days of the 19th-century French emperor Napoleon.

individualism a political philosophy that argues that individuals are most effective when they are responsible only for their own well-being and not for that of other members of society.

installment buying a method of buying originally introduced by car companies in the 1920s that allowed purchasers to make a downpayment on a purchase and then pay the balance in a series of regular installments.

isolationism an approach adopted in the United States after World War I that argued that the country should disassociate itself from affairs elsewhere in the world. It led to the U.S. failure to join the League of Nations.

Keynesianism the economic theory advocated by John Maynard Keynes in the 1920s and 1930s. Keynes argued that governments should spend money to maintain full employment and stimulate the economy. His theories dominated most western democracies from the 1930s to around the 1980s.

labor union a formal organization in which workers act collectively in order to protect their interests such as pay and work conditions.

laissez-faire a French term for "let it be," used to describe an economy with no government regulation of business activity. Laissez-faire is an important part of classical or free-market economics, which holds that laws of supply and demand alone should regulate prices, wages, and other economic factors.

liberalism a political theory that emphasizes a belief in progress, the autonomy of individuals, and the protection of political and civil rights; also an economic theory based on competition and the free market.

mixed economy an economy that combines characteristics of a free-market economy—competition, private ownership—with a limited amount of state involvement, such as regulation of business, wage and hour legislation, and a degree of nationalization.

mutualism a U.S. political tradition that advocates cooperative action as a way to lessen the negative social effects of the economy. The mutualist tradition was behind the general acceptance in the 1930s that government had an obligation to look after its citizens.

nativism an anti-immigrant U.S. political tradition that values "real" Americans and their attitudes over those of more recent immigrants. In the late 19th century nativism saw first- or second-generation Irish immigrants objecting to newcomers from southern Europe, for example.

planned economy an economy in which economic activity is controlled by the state. Most businesses are nationalized rather than privately owned, and the government sets production quotas, wages, and prices.

populism a name given to numerous political movements of the 1930s that claimed to represent the common people; populism also describes the beliefs of the Populist Party formed in 1891 to represent rural interests and the breakup of monopolies.

progressivism a political tradition in the United States that advocated social reform by government legislation. Both the Republican and Democratic parties had progressive wings.

public works projects often large-scale projects run by federal, state, or local government in order to generate employment.

recession a severe decline in economic activity that lasts for at least six months

regulation a word used to describe moves by government or other agencies to control business activity, such as by legislation relating to minimum wages or maximum working hours or health and safety procedures.

relief the term most often used in the 1920s and 1930s for welfare.

Social Darwinism a social theory based on the theory of natural selection proposed by Charles Darwin. Social Darwinists believed that some people inevitably became richer or more powerful than others, and that inequality was therefore acceptable.

socialism a political doctrine that removes business from private ownership in favor of state or cooperative ownership in order to create a more equitable society.

welfare financial or other help distributed to people in need; the word is also sometimes used to apply to the agencies that distribute the aid.

FURTHER READING

Allen, Frederick Lewis. *Since Yesterday: The 1930s in America, September 3, 1929–September 3, 1939.* New York: HarperCollins, 1986.

Brogan, Hugh. *The Penguin History of the United States of America.* New York: Penguin Books, 1990.

Evans, Harold. *The American Century.* New York: Knopf, 1999.

Handlin, Oscar, and Lilian Handlin. *Liberty and Equality: 1920–1994.* New York: HarperCollins Publishers, 1994.

Jones, M. A. *The Limits of Liberty: American History 1607–1992.* New York: Oxford University Press, 1995.

Kennedy, David M. *Freedom From Fear: The American People in Depression and War, 1929–1945* (Oxford History of the United States). New York: Oxford University Press, 1999.

Meltzer, Milton. *Brother Can You Spare a Dime?: The Great Depression 1929–1933* New York: Facts on File, Inc., 1991.

Nardo, Don (ed.). *The Great Depression* (Opposing Viewpoints Digest). Greenhaven Press, 1998.

Parrish, Michael E. *Anxious Decades: America in Prosperity and Depression, 1920–1941.* New York: W. W. Norton & Company Inc., 1994.

Phillips, Cabell. *From the Crash to the Blitz: 1929-1939.* Bronx, NY: Fordham University Press, 2000.

Watkins, T. H. *The Great Depression: America in the 1930s.* Boston: Little Brown and Co, 1995.

Worster, Donald. *Dust Bowl: The Southern Plains in the 1930s.* New York: Oxford University Press, 1982

NOVELS AND EYEWITNESS ACCOUNTS

Agee, James, and Walker Evans. *Let Us Now Praise Famous Men.* Boston: Houghton Mifflin Co., 2000

Burg, David F. *The Great Depression: An Eyewitness History.* New York: Facts on File, Inc., 1996

Caldwell, Erskine. *God's Little Acre.* Athens, GA: University of Georgia Press, 1995.

Caldwell, Erskine, and Margaret Bourke-White. *You Have Seen Their Faces.* Athens, GA: University of Georgia Press, 1995.

Dos Passos, John. *U.S.A.* New York: Library of America, 1996.

Farell, James T. *Studs Lonigan: A Trilogy.* Urbana: University of Illinois Press, 1993.

Faulkner, William. *Absalom, Absalom!* Boston: McGraw Hill College Division, 1972.

Hemingway, Ernest. *To Have and Have Not.* New York: Scribner, 1996.

———. *For Whom the Bell Tolls.* New York: Scribner, 1995.

Le Sueur, Meridel. *Salute to Spring.* New York: International Publishers Co., Inc., 1977.

McElvaine, Robert S. *Down and Out in the Great Depression: Letters from the Forgotten Man.* Chapel Hill, NC: University of North Carolina Press, 1983.

Olsen, Tillie. *Yonnondio: From the Thirties.* New York: Delta, 1979.

Smedley, Agnes. *Daughter of Earth: A Novel.* New York: Feminist Press, 1987.

Steinbeck, John. *The Grapes of Wrath.* New York: Penguin USA, 1992.

———. *Of Mice and Men.* New York: Penguin USA, 1993.

Terkel, Studs. *Hard Times: An Oral History of the Great Depression.* New York: The New Press, 2000.

Wright, Richard. *Native Son.* New York: HarperCollins, 1989.

PROLOGUE TO THE DEPRESSION

Allen, Frederick Lewis. *Only Yesterday.* New York: Harper and Brothers, 1931.

Bordo, Michael D., Claudia Goldin, and Eugene N. White (eds.). *The Defining Moment: The Great Depression and the American Economy in the Twentieth Century.* Chicago: University of Chicago Press, 1998.

Cohen, Lizabeth. *Making a New Deal.* New York: Cambridge University Press, 1990.

Galbraith, John Kenneth. *The Great Crash 1929.* Boston: Houghton Mifflin Co., 1997.

Kennedy, David M. *Over Here: The First World War and American Society.* New York: Oxford University Press, 1980.

Knock, T. J. *To End All Wars: Woodrow Wilson and the Quest for a New World Order.* Princeton, NJ: Princeton University Press.

Levian, J. R. *Anatomy of a Crash, 1929.* Burlington, VT: Fraser Publishing Co., 1997.

Sobel, Robert. *The Great Bull Market: Wall Street in the 1920s.* New York: W. W. Norton & Company Inc., 1968.

———. *Panic on Wall Street.* New York: Macmillan, 1968.

Wilson, Joan Hoff. *Herbert Hoover: Forgotten Progressive.* Boston: Little, Brown, 1975.

FDR AND OTHER INDIVIDUALS

Alsop, Joseph. *FDR: 1882–1945.* New York: Gramercy, 1998.

Brinkley, Alan. *Voices of Protest: Huey Long, Father Coughlin, and the Great Depression.* New York: Knopf, 1982.

Cook, Blanche Wiesen. *Eleanor Roosevelt: A Life.* New York: Viking, 1992.

Fried, Albert, *FDR and His Enemies.* New York: St. Martin's Press, 1999.

Graham, Otis L., Jr., and Meghan Wander (eds.) *Franklin D. Roosevelt, His Life and Times: An Encyclopedic View.* Boston: G.K. Hall & Co, 1985.

Hunt, John Gabriel, and Greg Suriano (eds.). *The Essential Franklin Delano Roosevelt: FDR's Greatest Speeches, Fireside Chats, Messages, and Proclamations.* New York: Gramercy, 1998.

Maney, Patrick J. *The Roosevelt Presence: The Life and Legacy of FDR.* Berkeley: University of California Press, 1998.

Roosevelt, Eleanor. *The Autobiography of Eleanor Roosevelt.* New York: Da Capo Press, 2000.

Watkins, T. H. *Righteous Pilgrim: The Life and Times of Harold L. Ickes.* New York: Henry Holt, 1990.

White, Graham. *Harold Ickes of the New Deal: His Private Life and Public Career.* Cambridge, MA: Harvard University Press, 1985.

SOCIAL HISTORY

Clausen, John A. *American Lives: Looking Back at the Children of the Great Depression.* Berkeley, CA: University of California Press, 1995.

Elder, Glen H., Jr. *Children of the Great Depression.* New York: HarperCollins, 1998.

Gregory, James N. *American Exodus: The Dust Bowl Migration and Okie Culture in California.* New York: Oxford University Press, 1991.

Katz, Michael B. *In the Shadow of the Poorhouse: A Social History of Welfare in America.* New York: Basic Books, 1997.

Lowitt, Richard, and Maurine Beasley (eds.). *One Third of a Nation: Lorena Hickok Reports on the Great Depression.* Urbana: University of Illinois Press, 1981.

McGovern, James R. *And a Time for Hope: Americans and the Great Depression.* Westport, CT: Praeger Publishers, 2000.

Patterson, James T. *America's Struggle Against Poverty: 1900–1980.* Cambridge, MA: Harvard University Press, 1981.

Starr, Kevin. *Endangered Dreams: The Great Depression in California* (Americans and the California Dream). New York: Oxford University Press, 1996.

Ware, Susan. *Holding the Line: American Women in the 1930s.* Boston: Twayne, 1982.

Weiss, Nancy. *Farewell to the Party of Lincoln: Black Politics in the Age of FDR.* Princeton: Princeton University Press, 1983.

CULTURE AND THE ARTS

Benet's Reader's Encyclopedia of American Literature. New York: Harpercollins, 1996.

Davidson, Abraham A. *Early American Modernist Painting, 1910–1935.* New York: Da Capo Press, 1994.

Haskell, Barbara. *The American Century: Art & Culture, 1900–1950.* New York: W. W. Norton & Co., 1999.

Hughes, Robert. *American Visions: The Epic History of Art in America.* New York: Knopf, 1999.

McJimsey, George. *Harry Hopkins: Ally of the Poor and Defender of Democracy.* Cambridge, Mass.: Harvard University Press, 1987.

Meltzer, Milton. *Violins and Shovels: The WPA Arts Projects.* New York: Delacorte Press, 1976.

———. *Dorothea Lange: A Photographer's Life.* Syracuse, NY: Syracuse University Press, 2000.

Pells, R. H. *Radical Visions and American Dreams: Culture and Social Thought in the Depression Years.* Urbana: Illinios University Press, 1998.

Pollack, Howard. *Aaron Copland: The Life and Work of an Uncommon Man.* New York: Henry Holt & Co., Inc., 1999.

Thomson, David. *Rosebud: The Story of Orson Welles.* New York: Vintage Books, 1997.

Wilson, Edmond. *The American Earthquake: A Document of the 1920s and 1930s.* Garden City, NY: Doubleday, 1958.

INTERNATIONAL AFFAIRS

Bullock, Alan. *Hitler: A Study in Tyranny.* New York: Harper and Row, 1962.

Dallek, Robert. *Franklin D. Roosevelt and American Foreign Policy.* New York: Oxford University Press, 1979.

Kindleberger, Charles P. *The World in Depression, 1929–1939.* Berkeley: University of California Press, 1986.

Offner, A. A. *The Origins of the Second World War: American Foreign Policy and World Politics.* Melbourne, FL: Krieger Publishing Company, 1986.

Pauley, B. F. *Hitler, Stalin, and Mussolini: Totalitarianism in the Twentieth Century.* Wheeling, IL: Harlan Davidson, 1997.

Ridley, J. *Mussolini.* New York: St. Martin's Press, 1998.

WEB SITES

African American Odyssey: The Depression, The New Deal, and World War II
http://lcweb2.loc.gov/ammem/aaohtml/exhibit/aopart8.html

America from the Great Depression to World War II: Photographs from the FSA and OWI, 1935–1945
http://memory.loc.gov/ammem/fsowhome.html

The American Experience: Surviving the Dust Bowl
http://www.pbs.org/wgbh/amex/dustbowl

Biographical Directory of the United States Congress
http://bioguide.congress.gov

By the People, For the People: Posters from the WPA, 1936–1943
http://memory.loc.gov/ammem/wpaposters/wpahome.html

Federal Theater Project
http://memory.loc.gov/ammem/fedtp/fthome.html

Huey Long
http://www.lib.lsu.edu/special/long.html

The New Deal Network, Franklin and Eleanor Roosevelt Institute
http://newdeal.feri.org

New York Times Archives
http://www.nytimes.com

Presidents of the United States
http://www.ipl.org/ref/POTUS.html

The Scottsboro Boys
http://www.english.upenn.edu/~afilreis/88/scottsboro.html

Voices from the Dust Bowl: The Charles L. Todd and Robert Sonkin Migrant Worker Collection, 1940–1941
http://memory.loc.gov/ammem/afctshtml/tshome.html

WPA American Life Histories
http://lcweb2.loc.gov/ammem/wpaintro/wpahome.html

PICTURE CREDITS

TIMELINE OF THE DEPRESSION

1929
Hoover creates Farm Board
Stock-market crash (October)

1930
California begins voluntary repatriation of Mexicans and Mexican Americans
Smoot-Hawley Tariff Act
Little Caesar, first great gangster movie of the sound era
Ford cuts workforce by 70 percent (June)
Drought strikes Midwest (September)

1931
Credit Anstalt, Austrian bank, collapses (May 1)
All German banks close (July 13)
Britain abandons gold standard (September 21)

1932
Norris-La Guardia Act
Congress approves Reconstruction Finance Corporation (January 22)
FDR makes "forgotten man" radio broadcast (April 7)
Repression of Bonus Expeditionary Force by Douglas MacArthur (June 17)
Farmers' Holiday Association organizes a farmers' strike (August)
FDR wins a landslide victory in presidential election (November 8)

1933
Fiorello La Guardia elected mayor of New York City.
Nazi leader Adolf Hitler becomes chancellor of Germany
Assassination attempt on FDR by Giuseppe Zangara (February 15)
FDR takes oath as 32nd president of the United States (March 4)
National bank holiday (March 6)
Start of the Hundred Days: Emergency Banking Relief Act (March 9)
FDR delivers first "fireside chat" (March 12)
Economy Act (March 20)
Beer-Wine Revenue Act (March 22)
Civilian Conservation Corps Reforestation Relief Act (March 31)
Emergency Farm Mortgage Act (May)
Federal Emergency Relief Act (FERA) and Agricultural Adjustment Administration (AAA) created (May 12)
Tennessee Valley Authority (May 18)
Federal Securities Act (May 27)
London Economic Conference (June)
Home Owners Refinancing Act (June 13)
Banking Act; Farm Credit Act; Emergency Railroad Transportation Act; National Industrial Recovery Act;

Glass Steagall Banking Act (June 16)
73rd Congress adjourns (June 16)
FDR creates Civil Works Administration (November)

1934
U.S. joins International Labour Organization
Huey Long launches Share-Our-Wealth Society (January)
Farm Mortgage Refinancing Act (January 31)
Securities Exchange Act (June 6)
National Housing Act (June 28)

1935
Emergency Relief Appropriation Act (April 8)
Soil Conservation Act (April 27)
Resettlement Administration created (May 1)
Rural Electrification Administration created (May 11)
Sureme Court rules NIRA unconstitutional (May 27)
Works Progress Administration formed (May 6)
Federal Music Project introduced (July)
National Labor Relations (Wagner) Act (July 5)
Social Security Act (August 14)
Banking Act (August 23)
Public Utility Holding Company Act (August 28)
Farm Mortgage Moratorium Act (August 29)
Revenue Act of 1935 (August 30)
Wealth Tax Act (August 31)
Huey Long dies after assassination (September 10)

1936
FDR wins 1936 election (November 3)
Gone with the Wind published
Charlie Chaplin's *Modern Times* is last great silent movie
Supreme Court rules AAA unconstitutional (January 6)
Soil Conservation and Domestic Allotment Act (1936) (February 29)
Voodoo Macbeth opens in New York (April 14)

1937
Wagner-Steagall National Housing Act (September 1)
Supreme Court axes NLRB
CIO wins a six-week sit-down strike at General Motors plant in Flint, Michigan.
Supreme Court Retirement Act (March 1)
Bituminous Coal Act (April 26)
Neutrality Act of 1937 (May 1)
Farm Tenant Act (July 22)

Revenue Act of 1937 (August 26)
National Housing Act (September 1)
Start of sit-down strike at General Motors Fisher Body Plant in Flint, Michigan, which lasts 44 days (December)

1938
Amended Federal Housing Act (February 4)
Agricultural Adjustment Act (1938) (February 16)
Naval Expansion Act of 1938 (May 17)
Revenue Act of 1938 (May 28)
Food, Drink, and Cosmetic Act (June 24)
Fair Labor Standards Act (June 25)
Orson Welles' *The War of the Worlds* broadcast (October 30)

1939
John Steinbeck's *The Grapes of Wrath* published
Public Works Administration discontinued
Federal Loan Agency created
Supreme Court declares the sit-down strike illegal (February 27)
Administrative Reorganization Act of 1939 (April 3)
Hatch Act (August 2)
Outbreak of World War II in Europe (September 3)
Neutrality Act of 1939 (November 4)

1940
In California the Relief Appropriation Act is passed, raising the period of eligibility for relief from one to three years
Richard Wright's *Native Son* establishes him as the era's leading black author

1941
American Guide series published for the last time
Publication of James Agee and Walker Evans' *Let Us Now Praise Famous Men*
Japanese bomb Pearl Harbor, Hawaii, bringing U.S. into World War II (December 7)

1943
Government eliminates all WPA agencies

1944
Farm Security Administration closed

1945
FDR dies
Japanese surrender

INDEX